Do I Fit the Color of the Rainbow?

Dr. John E. Bell

Do I Fit the Color of the Rainbow?

RiverHouse Publishing, LLC is registered in the United States Patent and Trademark Office.

All **RiverHouse, LLC** Titles, Imprints and Distributed Lines are available at special quantity discounts for bulk purchases for sales promotions, premiums, fund-raising and educational or institutional use.

Imprint: *RiverHouse Publishing, LLC*

ISBN: 978-09832186-3-0

Printed in the United States

This book is printed on acid-free paper.

Acknowledgments

I want to dedicate this book to my Daughter Amber and all my children that may be in the future. To my children, know that your Father has always loved you now and always. I want to thank my family and my Mother for her endless support of my work. I would like to thank all persons that have been in my corner since the start of my writing career. I also would like to give honor to River House Publishing LLC specifically, Mrs. Latrivia Nelson and all the staff and supporters that have been extremely gracious and kind to me, I thank you from the bottom of my heart. I want to give a special note to all who may face challenges in their personal lives. Never allow the turbulence of daily living to damage your Rainbow of thought. Always aspire to reach for the spiritual strength and calming space of peace in mind and soul; it is there that you will find a clear resolution to all matters. Allow God to grant you a great Rainbow of life so you can endure life's challenges and learn to love your own Color of the Rainbow.

Table of Contents

Chapter 1

Do I fit the Color of the Rainbow?

It is easy to ask how one fits into clothing or your favorite shoes or anything external to the soul of life that is without effort to put on or take off. But what happens when you have to ask yourself from within, "do you fit your life and what is happening to the life that you are now living?" Most experts agree that when the mirror of life is held up to most of us that most people do not like what they see. For example, most people will use all sorts of makeup, clothing or even alternative drugs to escape that feeling of being alone within their own skin or naked with the soul of themselves. It is true that reality can often be cruel to the innocent and the shallow of heart; however, it is the reality of our quiet time that we find out just who we really are and without that quiet scary and often dreadful silence within, we would not know our meaning of life's existence today.

I am on a mission in this book to look into the silence of the dead moments of life often referred to as the rainbow of goals in most people's lives. This dead space of thought or lonely silence produces most comedian's actors, doctors, scientist and even world leaders. This silence of a rainbow thoughts also predicts what types of friends one will attract what type of lover one seeks in the night and how the taboo of the mind and spirit often wrestle for the reality spot light of control for gratification of passionate satisfaction.

The reality of the silence is very real and controls the subconscious through dreams or visions and even goal setting and often short goal attainment that will build the dead space in confidence of what the life of an individual will eventually become. This can be everything from a president of a nation to the serial killer that perils a community into fear with terror.

It becomes a part of everyone's daily existence to know their own silence of a rainbow of thoughts that will guide themselves toward ultimate happiness and peace in the walk of life that every living individual must make. The question becomes, "what does one do with the energy and moments that are encountered in the dead silence amongst the rainbow of thoughts that only the soul of an individual can direct and only from within?" This question is only answered by an individual that is totally in tune with their thoughts and where those thoughts are coming from; how those thoughts are entertained and by whom the thoughts in silence can be controlled. The Rainbow of thoughts can be influenced by lovers, friends, spouses and even children.

In fact, most people agree that the media and the news of the day often control what the silence in the rainbow of thoughts utter in the darkness with the mirror of yourself only to evaluate its extremes of influence in your life. Ironically, with this knowledge now well known of how we are all influenced by news and the media, what do we choose in our lives to be our own reality?

This is a unique question as we ponder and evaluate the rainbow of thoughts in the silence within our souls. This will enhance our daily mission of paying bills running errands and finding the perfect exercise equipment to give us the six pack abs that most people will never have in their lifetimes. Consequently, it seems that without this silence of a rainbow of thoughts we would only be fat slobs of a society merely living for the TV and the videos to show us how to live and even spend money and who to marry and unfortunately, even how to divorce.

Therefore, it is an absolute necessity that we have the silence of thought in life to keep our minds focused on what we need to do to meet our goals and accomplish our dreams in life. As we look at the dead silence of the rainbow of thoughts within let us make sure that we are mature enough to handle what we find in ourselves and what really lies beneath our make-up, hair weave, drugs an even appetites for food as a friend and not nourishment of the body.

The inner soul is made up of many unforeseen events of the past and present that most people have been influenced by their whole lives and would never know it. Many have never waited even for a day to visit within to hear the cries, joys and even the pains of the soul to make good decisions from those experiences. Instead, most people mentally block out the negative in the conscious mind in order to focus on the future or present day living and make their choices from these experiences.

This can be survival of the fittest or it can also be to run away from the dead silence that is unknown to the mind or even misunderstood by the person that is afraid to encounter themselves. Most people prefer not to discover that hidden point of life that fear alone entraps them from discovering. Addictions are often easier to deal with believe it or not than the fear of one's own rainbow of thought.

So many readers will read this book and wonder in fear to themselves do they live a lie or do they live at all. The truth is most people exist and very little living is ever done at all because most people are consumed with consumerism and not conventional freedom of thought itself.

For example, why is there such a feeling of desperation and hopelessness in urban youth today? It seems that most of them are consumed by media hype fashion videos, violence and sexual satisfaction without maturity of the reality of the action in sexual molestation or statutory rape due to the perversion of sexual images from early on in their lives.

These images are noted from experience in many cases and often with the influence of videos that many urban youth consider attractive and stimulating to watch as young men and woman gyrate their bodies to music. This stimulates the young mind into thoughts that the body of many young kids are not ready for but are eager to attempt with great passion due to peer pressure and self driven thoughts of sexual pleasure. Ironically, kids are misguided by societal cultural norms of urban acceptance that helps self-destruction of the young urban mind today.

Unfortunately, it is no surprise to note why African-Americans have the highest dropout rate from high school today by 38% in most urban cities in the US alone and the highest homicide rate by 77% and worst the greatest HIV infection rate amongst all youth ages 13-25 especially seen in females today. So it is known that we are observing that the dead silence of the rainbow thoughts are totally ignored from within in our urban youth in the US.

Meanwhile, the garbage of the media continuously plays dead music and terrorist style consumer franchise liquor stores, fast food and drugs invade the urban community to rape its youth of their inner thought from the rainbow of possibilities that only from within they can solve these issues of the day.

The greatest crime of humanity is to rob oneself of the inner rainbow of thoughts from the silence within the soul. I cannot say who orchestrated the demise of the urban community but whoever it is they are a genius. Fortunately, it has not affected the Asian community or the White community or even the Indian community.

Most of their communities are clean and self maintained by their own tax dollars and most of their communities have their own schools and municipalities that govern their neighborhoods.

Case and point, I have never seen a drug store in an affluent White, Indian or Asian neighborhood nor have I ever seen videos intentionally made to denigrate their women or glorify ignorance of their cultural heritage as the urban community has embraced the ignorance of our state of life as a sign of allegiance.

This unlikely brotherhood is built around economic failure and Government control of where we live, lack of education, to the jail life that many try to make into a fashion statement with the low drawers pants and gang paraphernalia. Sadly, as I have tried to interview many participants of these soul less in thought folks; the conversation is dismal and void of thought as if someone has taken their very soul or worst the capable brain of this individual all together. Ironically, this to me is the ultimate terrorist act gone right by the mental disfranchisement of many urban youth today.

This urgency then summons the call of all educated persons of society African-American, White, Asian and Indian populations to try a new way to unlock the robbed consciousness of the urban youth today. I have found that we need the urban youth because they are outnumbering our well educated members in society and unfortunately it is not sexy in society to continue to build prisons and drug rehab institutions.

We cannot substantiate the logic of being the only world super power with the greatest incarceration rate of any industrialize nation of the face of the earth. Besides, it is only to our discredit when we cannot show the world optimal opportunities with equal education and health care then America becomes the laughing stock of the world.

Today, we have an increased amount of less educated citizens than many other industrialize nations in the world. This becomes the stain of America that has a deep root in Jim Crow laws from the nineteen fifties and even the cultural bigotry noted in the south but also widely known in the Northern US as well. Over the last decade we have seen two war theatres in existence in the United States, the war in Afghanistan and Iraq, both wars have exhausted military and civilians alike.

Who will replace these soldiers if the generation of the rainbow of conscious thought is robbed from well disciplined educated men and women that the US will need to clean up the military mess that deranged, narcissistic political leaders began for power? These leaders often use the military as a personal attack dog in foreign affairs instead of America's true military force for protection in America's territory and constitutional standing in the world.

It is often our leaders both elected and appointed that have truly abandoned the silence of the rainbow of thought. However, because of their positions of authority the world is held captive by negative influences that can be infiltrated to sway national agendas and international campaigns. These agendas can promote war and not stability or peace in the democracy of opportunity and human freedom of thought in the world. Therefore, it is paramount that as we evaluate the silence of the rainbow of thought that we consider who is affected by the lack of this thought process. Moreover, who benefits in society when a segment of the minority citizens do not think clearly about their future standing in the world?

Chapter 2

What is a Freed African-American (minority) life worth in the year 2011?

It seems that minorities are just what the definition implies minor, insignificant and in some cases even invisible to the greater concerns of citizens of society today. Even with the social media and other fascinating technology gadgets of today in 2011, society is as isolated now as it was in the days of the Jim Crow era. Even now one can text, email and even teleconference their lives via the internet and never engage all of society. Yet, life goes on as long as Wall Street maintains its value and cash is king and electric currency continues to move in the society from one extreme to another.

The minority citizen will always be last in this paradigm of society because of the lack of freedom of thought to compete in this new age technology challenge that continues to entrap most under educated men and women today. Many minority youth are competitive yet culturally robbed of the freedom of creative thought by failing schools and poor educational standards. This unique trap is not new; it is the same mechanism of philosophy that has been used for decades and it is so simple that most minorities are yet convinced that it is all powerful over their lives today. In-fact, it has nothing to do with being White, Indian, Asian or African-American. The trap was started over 200 hundred years ago by a Man named Willie Lynch. An infamous speech is credited to this unique figure of urban history and his authenticity is in debate. There were other infamous people credited for lynching laws by likes of Captain William Lynch (1742-1820) who lead a caravan of men that lynched opposing White men and Blacks in public fashion to instill terror and instituted the lynch laws in Virginia. One other infamous person by the last name of Lynch is Judge Charles Lynch of Virginia that carried lynching on Whites in Virginia Tories communities. Some historian's credit's the term Lynching to his terror tactics of 1814-1826.

All of these men share this evil terror tactic that has affected multiple generations. However, Willie Lynch was a genius terrorist strategist that many American Slave masters heard about and needed help to prevent slave revolutions and revolting against authority. Willie Lynch's documented speech on December 25, 1712 is the most referenced document many African-American historians refer as the mental strategy that systematically destroyed African-American culture.

Evidence of Willie Lynch or even the speech has prompted debate but the philosophy and doctrine is known all too well in today's African-American society. This doctrine has changed African-American culture significantly by instituting the terror tactic lynching which it gets its name from the pioneer of lynching.

The doctrine implies that the Nigger (slave) is not good enough for human recognition and you have to make them hate against themselves to out do the other Nigger (slaves) of dark complexion by degrading or devaluing their neighbor who is their competitor for some recognition of the slave master to keep control of the slaves on the plantation.

I have placed the speech in its entirety in the chapter not to delete or add to this terrorist doctrine or philosophy that has systematically destroyed the minds of many African-American generations.

The Willie Lynch Letter: The Making of a Slave!

This speech was delivered by Willie Lynch on the bank of the James River in the colony of Virginia in 1712. Lynch was a British slave owner in the West Indies. He was invited to the colony of Virginia in 1712 to teach his methods to slave owners there. The term "lynching" is derived from his last name.

December 25, 1712

Gentlemen:

I greet you here on the bank of the James River in the year of our Lord one thousand seven hundred and twelve. First, I shall thank you, the gentlemen of the Colony of Virginia, for bringing me here. I am here to help you solve some of your problems with slaves. Your invitation reached me on my modest plantation in the West Indies, where I have experimented with some of the newest and still the oldest methods for control of slaves. Ancient Rome's would envy us if my program is implemented. As our boat sailed south on the James River, named for our illustrious King, whose version of the Bible we cherish, I saw enough to know that your problem is not unique. While Rome used cords of wood as crosses for standing human bodies along its highways in great numbers, you are here using the tree and the rope on occasions. I caught the whiff of a dead slave hanging from a tree, a couple miles back. You are not only losing valuable stock by hangings, you are having uprisings, and slaves are running away, your crops are sometimes left in the fields too long for maximum profit, you suffer occasional fires, and your animals are killed. Gentlemen, you know what your problems are; I do not need to elaborate. I am not here to enumerate your problems; I am here to introduce you to a method of solving them. In my bag here, I have a foolproof method for controlling your black slaves. I guarantee every one of you that if installed correctly it will control the slaves for at least 300 years [2012]. My method is simple. Any member of your family or your overseer can use it. I have outlined a number of differences among the slaves and make the differences bigger. I use fear, distrust and envy for control. These methods have worked on my modest plantation in the West Indies and it will work throughout the South. Take this simple little list of differences and think about them. On top of my list is "age" but it's there only because it starts with an "A." The second is "COLOR" or shade, there is intelligence, size, sex, size of plantations and status on plantations, attitude of owners, whether the slaves live in the valley, on a hill, East, West, North, South, have fine hair, course hair, or is tall or short. Now that you have a list of differences, I shall give you an outline of action, but before that, I shall assure you that distrust is stronger than trust and envy stronger than adulation, respect or admiration. The Black slaves after receiving this indoctri-

nation shall carry on and will become self refueling and self generating for hundreds of years, maybe thousands. Don't forget you must pitch the old black Male vs. the young black Male, and the young black Male against the old black male. You must use the dark skin slaves vs. the light skin slaves, and the light skin slaves vs. the dark skin slaves. You must use the female vs. the male. And the male vs. the female. You must also have you white servants and overseers distrust all Blacks. It is necessary that your slaves trust and depend on us. They must love, respect and trust only us. Gentlemen, these kits are your keys to control. Use them. Have your wives and children use them, never miss an opportunity. If used intensely for one year, the slaves themselves will remain perpetually distrustful of each other. Thank you gentlemen

Let's Make a Slave

It was the interest and business of slave holders to study human nature, and the slave nature in particular, with a view to practical results. I and many of them attained astonishing proficiency in this direction. They had to deal not with earth, wood and stone, but with men and by every regard they had for their own safety and prosperity they needed to know the material on which they were to work. Conscious of the injustice and wrong they were every hour perpetuating and knowing what they themselves would do. Were they the victims of such wrongs? They were constantly looking for the first signs of the dreaded retribution. They watched, therefore with skilled and practiced eyes, and learned to read with great accuracy, the state of mind and heart of the slave, through his sable face. Unusual sobriety, apparent abstractions, sullenness and indifference indeed, any mood out of the common was afforded ground for suspicion and inquiry. Let us make a slave. What do we need? First of all we need a black nigger man, a pregnant nigger woman and her baby nigger boy. Second, we will use the same basic principle that we use in breaking a horse, combined with some more sustaining factors. What we do with horses is that we break them from one form of life to another that is we reduce them from their natural state in nature. Whereas nature provides them with the natural capacity to take care of their offspring,

We break that natural string of independence from them and thereby create a dependency status, so that we may be able to get from them useful production for our business and pleasure

Cardinal Principles for making a Negro

For fear that our future Generations may not understand the principles of breaking both of the beasts together, the nigger and the horse. We understand that short range planning economics results in periodic economic chaos; so that to avoid turmoil in the economy, it requires us to have breadth and depth in long range comprehensive planning, articulating both skill sharp perceptions. We lay down the following principles for long range comprehensive economic planning. Both horse and niggers is no good to the economy in the wild or natural state. Both must be broken and tied together for orderly production. For orderly future, special and particular attention must be paid to the female and the youngest offspring. Both must be crossbred to produce a variety and division of labor. Both must be taught to respond to a peculiar new language. Psychological and physical instruction of containment must be created for both. We hold the six cardinal principles as truth to be self evident, based upon the following the discourse concerning the economics of breaking and tying the horse and the nigger together, all inclusive of the six principles laid down about.

NOTE: Neither principle alone will suffice for good economics. All principles must be employed for orderly good of the nation. Accordingly, both a wild horse and a wild or nature nigger is dangerous even if captured, for they will have the tendency to seek their customary freedom, and in doing so, might kill you in your sleep. You cannot rest. They sleep while you are awake, and are awake while you are asleep. They are dangerous near the family house and it requires too much labor to watch them away from the house.

Above all, you cannot get them to work in this natural state. Hence both the horse and the nigger must be broken; that is breaking them from one form of mental life to another. Keep the body take the mind! In other words break the will to resist. Now the breaking process is the same for both the horse and the nigger, only slightly varying in degrees. But as we said before, there is an art in long range economic planning. You must keep your eye and thoughts on the female and the offspring of the horse and the nigger. A brief discourse in offspring development will shed light on the key to sound economic principles. Pay little attention to the generation of original breaking, but concentrate on future generations. Therefore, if you break the female mother, she will break the offspring in its early years of development and when the

Offspring is old enough to work; she will deliver it up to you, for her normal female protective tendencies will have been lost in the original breaking process. For example take the case of the wild stud horse, a female horse and an already infant horse and compare the breaking process with two captured nigger males in their natural state, a pregnant nigger woman with her infant offspring. Take the stud horse, break him for limited containment. Completely break the female horse until she becomes very gentle, whereas you or anybody can ride her in her comfort.

Breed the mare and the stud until you have the desired offspring. Then you can turn the stud to freedom until you need him again. Train the female horse whereby she will eat out of your hand, and she will in turn train the infant horse to eat out of your hand also. When it comes to breaking the uncivilized nigger, use the same process, but vary the degree and step up the pressure, so as to do a complete reversal of the mind.

Take the meanest and most restless nigger, strip him of his clothes in front of the remaining male niggers, the female, and the nigger infant, tar and feather him, tie each leg to a different horse faced in opposite directions, set him a fire and beat both horses to pull him apart in front of the remaining nigger. The next step is to take a bull whip and beat the remaining nigger male to the point of death, in front of the female and the infant. Don't kill him, but put the fear of God in him, for he can be useful for future breeding.

The Breaking Process of the African Woman

Take the female and run a series of tests on her to see if she will submit to your desires willingly. Test her in every way, because she is the most important factor for good economics. If she shows any sign of resistance in submitting completely to your will, do not hesitate to use the bull whip on her to extract that last bit of resistance out of her. Take care not to kill her, for in doing so, you spoil well economic.

When in complete submission, she will train her off springs in the early years to submit to labor when they become of age. Understanding is the best thing. Therefore, we shall go deeper into this area of the subject matter concerning what we have produced here in this breaking process of the female nigger.

We have reversed the relationship in her natural uncivilized state she would have a strong dependency on the uncivilized nigger male, and she would have a limited protective tendency toward her independent male offspring and would raise male off springs to be dependent like her. Nature had provided for this type of balance.

We reversed nature by burning and pulling a civilized nigger apart and bull whipping the other to the point of death, all in her presence. By her being left alone, unprotected, with the male image destroyed, the ordeal caused her to move from her psychological dependent state to a frozen independent state. In this frozen psychological state of independence, she will raise her male and female offspring in reversed roles.

For fear of the young males life she will psychologically train him to be mentally weak and dependent, but physically strong. Because she has become psychologically independent, she will train her female off springs to be psychological independent.

What have you got? You've got the nigger women out front and the nigger man behind and scared. This is a perfect situation of sound sleep and economic. Before the breaking process, we had to be alertly on guard at all times.

Now we can sleep soundly, for out of frozen fear his woman stands guard for us. He cannot get past her early slave molding process. He is a good tool, now ready to be tied to the horse at a tender age. By the time a nigger boy reaches the age of sixteen, he is soundly broken in and ready for a long life of sound and efficient work and the reproduction of a unit of good labor force.

Continually through the breaking of uncivilized savage nigger, by throwing the nigger female savage into a frozen psychological state of independence, by killing of the protective male image, and by creating a submissive dependent mind of the nigger male slave, we have created an orbiting cycle that turns on its own axis forever, unless a phenomenon occurs and re shifts the position of the male and female slaves. We show what we mean by example. Take the case of the two economic slave units and examine them closely.

The Nigger Marriage

We breed two nigger males with two nigger females. Then we take the nigger males away from them and keep them moving and working. Say one nigger female bears a nigger female and the other bears a nigger male. Both nigger females being without influence of the nigger male image, frozen with an independent psychology, will raise their offspring into reverse positions. The one with the female offspring will teach her to be like herself, independent and negotiable (we negotiate with her, through her, by her, we negotiate her at will). The one with the nigger male offspring, she being frozen with a subconscious fear for his life, will raise him to be mentally dependent and weak, but physically strong, in other words, body over mind. Now in a few years when these two offspring's become fertile for early reproduction we will mate and breed them and continue the cycle. That is good, sound, and long range comprehensive planning.

Warning: Possible Interloping Negatives

Earlier we talked about the non economic good of the horse and the nigger in their wild or natural state; we talked out the principle of breaking and tying them together for orderly production. Furthermore, we talked about paying particular attention to the female savage and her offspring for orderly future planning, and then more recently we stated that, by reversing the positions of the male and female savages, we created an orbiting cycle that turns on its own axis forever unless a phenomenon occurred and resift and positions of the male and female savages.

Our experts warned us about the possibility of this phenomenon occurring, for they say that the mind has a strong drive to correct and re-correct itself over a period of time if I can touch some substantial original historical base, and they advised us that the best way to deal with the phenomenon is to shave off the brute's mental history and create a multiplicity of phenomena of illusions, so that each illusion will twirl in its own orbit, something similar to floating balls in a vacuum.

This creation of multiplicity of phenomena of illusions entails the principle of crossbreeding the nigger and the horse as we stated above, the purpose of which is to create a diversified division of labor thereby creating different levels of labor and different values of illusion at each connecting level of labor. The results of which is the severance of the points of original beginnings for each sphere illusion.

Since we feel that the subject matter may get more complicated as we proceed in laying down our economic plan concerning the purpose, reason and effect of crossbreeding horses and nigger, we shall lay down the following definition terms for future generations. Orbiting cycle means a thing turning in a given path. Axis means upon which or around which a body turns. Phenomenon means something beyond ordinary conception and inspires awe and wonder.

Multiplicity means a great number. Sphere means a globe. Cross breeding a horse means taking a horse and breeding it with an ass and you get a dumb backward ass long headed mule that is neither reproductive nor productive by itself. Crossbreeding niggers mean taking so many drops of good white blood and putting them into as many nigger women as possible, varying the drops by the various tones that you want, and then letting them breed with each other until another cycle of color appears as you desire.

What this means is this; put the niggers and the horse in a breeding pot, mix some assess and some good white blood and what do you get? You got a multiplicity of colors of ass backward, unusual niggers, running, tied to a backward ass long headed mule, the one productive of itself, the other sterile. (The one constant, the other dying, we keep the nigger constant for we may replace the mules for another tool) both mule and nigger tied to each other, neither knowing where the other came from and neither productive for itself, nor without each other.

Control the Language

Crossbreeding completed, for further severance from their original beginning, we must completely annihilate the mother tongue of both the new nigger and the new mule and institute a new language that involves the new life's work of both. You know language is a peculiar institution. It leads to the heart of a people. The more a foreigner knows about the language of another country the more he is able to move through all levels of that society. Therefore, if the foreigner is an enemy of the country, to the extent that he knows the body of the language, to that extent is the country vulnerable to attack or invasion of a foreign culture.

For example, if you take a slave, if you teach him all about your language, he will know all your secrets, and he is then no more a slave, for you can't fool him any longer. For example, if you told a slave that he must perform in getting out "our crops" and he knows the language well, he would know that "our crops" didn't mean "our crops" and the slavery system would break down, for he would relate on the basis of what "our crops" really meant. So you have to be careful in setting up the new language for the slaves would soon be in your house, talking to you "man to man" and that is death to our economic system.

In addition, the definitions of words or terms are only a minute part of the process. Values are created and transported by communication through the body of the language. A total society has many interconnected value system. All the values in the society have bridges of language to connect them for orderly working in the society. But for these language bridges, these many value systems would sharply clash and cause internal strife or civil war, the degree of the conflict being determined by the magnitude of the issues or relative opposing strength in whatever form.

For example, if you put a slave in a hog pen and train him to live there and incorporate in him to value it as a way of life completely, the biggest problem you would have out of him is that he would worry you about provisions to keep the hog pen clean, or the same hog pen and make a slip and incorporate something in his language whereby he comes to value a house more than he does his hog pen, you got a problem. He will soon be in your house. [The Willie Lynch Doctrine 1712]

Lynch's methods in the early 1800s and began to rape and treat light skin slaves better than dark skinned slaves and made the lighter slaves and the more attractive European looking slaves a second class citizen a step above the more Afro-centric looking kinky haired slaves in the field who did the hard labor and was usually the slaves that happen to revolt more than the fair skinned slaves that lived in better housing quarters and usually became the mistresses of the Slave masters according to many historical documents from this period of the indoctrination of slavery.

As you may know already from the Historical documents of the mid 1700s to the late 1800s, there was a revolution of time in history where the question was asked even by the US Statesmen of the day that were to frame the United States constitution itself.

The question was, "What is an African slave (minority) life worth compared to land property and human recognition according to European American newly developed territorial citizenry of the United States of America?" It is recognized even in the US constitution that all African born slaves even after being brought to the shores of the US were considered US property of the said slave owners and even passed down in wills and secured to a plantations for life.

Ultimately, the US constitution felt that to keep the African slave as property that they could not be categorized as human so it was Thomas Jefferson and George Washington and many others that owned slaves that agreed that African citizens would be considered 3/5 human and recognized as cattle to the slave owner who purchased them at the price of the day due to the labor they could produce and age of the said African Slave (minority) at the time of purchase.

Credibly, this is all documented in the US constitution today so if any US citizen wanted to look it up, please do. This would demonstrate the concept why the minority life today is yet trapped in its philosophy of non entitlement in fairness by the actual Government that afforded the American standards of this particular rainbow of thought of the day.

Fortunately, this travesty was amended by the 13th amendment and the 14th amendment. However, not every state of the union respected these amendments and in some states freed African slaves needed to show papers to show that they were considered free or granted freedom even under these amendments of the day.

Recognizing that at this time in history that only about 60% of the White and 7% of the African citizen population were literate at this time in history. Slavery and the tactics of slavery was in acted by most White citizens and surprisingly even freed African slaves that became landowners and entrepreneurs owned slaves as well. This was over a hundred years after Willie Lynch's doctrine and even the US constitution backed this labor free work force. Everyone had a hand in slavery's lucrative benefits of the day, even freed African slaves themselves assisted with the terrorist thinking for many years after the 13th amendment passed. Consequently, old habits of ignorance and defiance of created superiority is hard to break after a hundred years of enjoyment from other African slaves (minority citizens) degradation.

Eventually, it was the honorable President Abraham Lincoln who signed and passed in 1865 the Emancipation Proclamation act that freed all slaves by law in the United States. Adversely, by then it was evident that the damage orchestrated by Willie Lynch was totally believed, indoctrinated and even culturally ratified at one time by the United States Constitution for almost one hundred years.

At this time in history, the US constitution disapproved of the cultural demoralization of life in America that directly affected African slaves that were now legally supposed to be free. However, no one was culturally prepared or financially ready to obey the law of the land. Ironically, the penalty for breaking the law was left up to the states that followed the law. But very few states at this time would cut off the provisions of self made wealth and prosperity due to free labor by a mere African citizen that was considered only 3/5 of a White human being.

Unfortunately even after the 13th amendment and 14th amendment and the 1865 Emancipation Proclamation, it would take almost 100 years to give freed African-American Citizens the legal right to vote and full legal rights to ownership of property housing and land throughout the south that had been handed down by law to former slaves on plantations for generations. This would be the 1965 civil rights bill orchestrated by the

Civil rights movement notably Dr. Martin L. King Jr. and many other notable leaders of the SCLC of the day along the honorable President John F. Kennedy.

Sadly, he would not live to see this very life altering legislation passed to change the cultural abnormality of the day that had existed at this time for more than 188 years since the original US constitution was drafted by the founding fathers of the United States that declared the African-American citizen 3/5 human compared to their White counterpart.

This is all documented in American history and can be easily researched so no one should be offended. However, I do not believe that the cultural effect on the mental and psychological parameters of cultural laws and legislation of the US Government on the lives of freed African-American minorities in America has ever been totally studied. I can only take on this challenge from my own 40 years of research of how I was impacted by these laws and legislation and how it has affected my life. Considerably, I mean my family's life and African-American lives as a whole that I know all too well.

Most freed African-American citizens can understand the pains and triumphs of the struggle to be recognized by the US Government that once imprisoned, enslaved and misrepresented these citizens; quite frankly, continues to under appreciate the survival and contributions of freed African-Americans (minorities) in history.

I say this because it is difficult to see African-Americans even in today's history books that are taught in schools. It is almost foreign to many freed African-American(minority) citizens today about the 3/5 human written statement in the US constitution or that the founding fathers owned slaves and even Thomas Jefferson himself had a mistress who was a African Slave woman named Sally Hemings, that abided in his quarters who he actually fathered children with. Why is this not in the school books?

Why are the states and Governments that fought and died over the right to keep Willie lynches doctrine alive called, "states right bill of the Southern Confederacy" not in every history school book in America? Why do you have to go and research about the free slave labor that was so abundant that the proclamation emancipation outlined 40 acres and a mule to every freed African-American citizen of the day. Special Order 15 from General William Tecumesh Sherman January 16, 1865, designated land of 40 acres and a mule to newly freed African slaves that joined the Union army during the Civil War. The designated land covered states of South Carolina, Georgia to the tip of the state of Florida, a sort of reparation of slavery due to the proclamation emancipation act. The land measured 400,000 acres for Union Army newly freed African-American men and their families.

Sadly, President Andrew Johnson, one year later in 1866 reversed this order and federally ordered land in South Carolina and Georgia of 400,000 acres be returned from African-American freed (Minority) citizens to former White Slave Owners. This US Government travesty occurred but I have never read it in any historical school book but it is Government record. The US Emancipation Proclamation act of 1865 was signed by the Honorable President Abraham Lincoln himself.

I guess the way America chooses not to acknowledge this stain in our country's history is to act like it never existed. Almost like the Greeks did the history of the

Great Egyptians, just don't recognize the contributions from their Egyptian masters that most Greeks emulated and based their way of Government after but not recognizing the lives of the ancient Egyptian Kings and Queens that ruled centuries before them on record even today.

It is amazing what most people think of the American style of cultural insignificance toward freed African-Americans (minorities) that has helped to frame the glorification of ignorance and miss-education and socio-economic disempowerment over the freed African-American (minority) today.

I can see how many institutions have helped to entrap the minds of the freed African-Americans (minorities) today. Many people are yet culturally indoctrinated that dark African skin is yet undervalued and light or fair skin is still more culturally valued today even after two hundred years of Willie Lynch. This cultural phenomenon is yet alive and well within the freed African-American consciousness today.

Many freed African-American men seek after features that resemble fair skinned or high European features in freed African-American woman today. This look is genetically enhanced by what many African-American men like which is natural less kinky long hair with keen features that look African-American; but, has the color and allure of the European skin complexion, that look to almost make the grade of the White woman today. Moreover, these African-American women can still pass the Negro color barrier and get the you can bring her into the house with the rest of us colored folk nod.

Many people yet endure this who are of mixed heritage but are genetically mixed with African-American blood but have White ancestry that is clearly apparent. It was almost considered a blessing if a freed African-American (minority) woman had a child that was considered mixed or just looked more like a genetically endowed baby that many people both White and African-American (minority) could see the European features in. Those children became the child stars and even selected for educational programs and movie parts and could actually get hired as secretaries and house maids more frequently than the more Afro-centric kinky haired and wide nosed African-American women of that time. More African features presented were considered an ugly thing at one time by freed African-Americans (minorities) and White citizens as well.

This knowledge dates back to the mid 1800s and even today in some small ignorant places where uninformed freed African-American (minorities) and some Whites and other nationalities yet live today. I am so glad that in the year 2011 that after two hundred years since the abandoned Willie Lynch laws, Jim Crow laws and the passage of the 1965 civil rights movement including the death of so many prominent members of our society; that we are not impacted any longer by the ugly negative cultural indoctrinated abnormalities of the years gone by. Sarcastically, I am aware from my own existence to know that is not totally true, unfortunately.

In 2011, there is yet degradation of our freed African-American (minority) women and men by the imagery of seduction in sex which is the highest drive of satisfaction with many African-American men especially. This can be imagined by the music that glorifies whoredom instead of mature sexual knowledge of freed African-American (minority) women of today.

In contrast, African-American women (minorities) actually obtain higher education degrees than most of their African-American (minority) male counterparts by over 27% according to the US census of 2010. How can our music and cultural phenomenon clash with the mediocrity of today's acceptance of a lack of education and the acceptance of low goals and Government empowerment and no personal entrepreneurial aspirations of business ownership?

This is a total contrast of the civil rights movement and even the strives made during the years following the 13th amendment of the US constitution. What happened to the consciousness of progressive African-American (minority) upward mobility toward success that we have struggled so hard to obtain collectively as a people? Ironically, it has been almost two hundred years since the Willie Lynch indoctrination of internal destruction of the African-American culture that many have fought so hard to change over our two hundred year struggle for freedom and respect in this nation. It seems that as we look at the question of what an African-American (minority) life is worth today?

One has to look at the incarceration rate that affects 77% of the African-American (minority) male population in the US alone. It is estimated that for every five freed African-American (minority) males born in 2011 that one out of every five will be imprisoned, impacted by domestic and gun violence. Unfortunately, even contribute to the drug infestation of America and now can be victims of rape by another man according to the Crime statistics report of 2010 and the US prison records statistics of 1995-2010 that is public record.

In fact, according to the US Census of 2010 there are for the first time in American History more freed African-American (minority) males in prison than there are in schools or college, please look it up. This does not take into affect that according to the disease statistics of the US Center of Disease control(CDC) that most cases of HIV/AIDS is found in the populations that are between 14-26 years of age. Consequently, today's freed African-American (minority) populations have negatively affected mostly African-American (minority) women. Unfortunately, this phenomenon is also escalated by freed African-American (minority) men who get raped by men or are seduced by other down low freed African-American (minority) men.

Most of these males are infected with the HIV/AIDS virus are habitual offenders of the law and revolve their lives between prison and street life. Sadly, these are the bad boys and the exciting cultural thugs of our society. Today's thugs, are the in thing to sexually experiment with according to some mis-informed young teens and adult freed African-American(minority) women of today.

Quite frankly, these women love the cultural ignorance and the low uneducated phenomenal freed African-American males that are dominating society today. This can be heard on any radio station or seen on any industry driven TV video station in America in 2011. Consequently, this is the accepted cultural norm not conjured by Whites like in Willie Lynch's case to mentally shackle the mind and physicality of freed and non-freed African-American(minority) populations; unfortunately, this degradation is committed by freed African-Americans(minorities) without any federal government over sight at all.

Emphatically, it is only to maintain the progressive subliminal degradation that the Government will allow for control of the silence of the rainbow of thought of most freed African-American (minorities). This keeps the offspring of this group under educational disenfranchisement with a lack of federal funding for progressive entrepreneurial aspiration. This enables a disconnect from political awareness of the US Government. Most historical sociological researchers know that the uneducated freed African-American (minority) is an ethnic population that in one hundred more years will be inherently enslaved all over again if the current trend continues with the educational dropout rate as high as 40 % in some urban cities in the United States.

The incarceration rate at 82% of freed African-American males that have less than a 8th grade education and ultimately the gun violent rate of death impacting about 78% of all freed African-American (minority) males and females, today.

Finally, the cultural norm of 71% of all African-American children born in 2011 to unmarried families and the accepted cultural norm of fatherless bastard children is an accepted norm since the late sixties and have not changed much since the post slavery days of the Jim Crow and Willie Lynch doctrines that has culturally devalued and destroyed more cultures and generations than any civil war or plague could ever destroy.

Paraphrasing Willie Lynch, "If you destroy their minds with acts of terror and enforce one over the other and make them turn on each other they will kill each other and self regulate themselves where all you have to do is select who you want to have the privilege to be the target ones of favor to make all others want what another

Nigger has and all will be well with your plantation and the Nigger slave will abide with this doctrine as long as you enforce its power over the Nigger slave," (Willie Lynch doctrine, 1712).

One of history's geniuses of US domestic terror that unfortunately many freed African-American (minorities) have not been able to mentally overcome even with the 13th and 14th amendment laws on the US Constitutional books and a Presidential blood bought civil rights bill of 1965. It is this awareness that many freed African-Americans feel when they are in African-American neighborhoods and have to be aware of their surroundings all the time and often feel on edge.

It is the obvious site of destruction and degradation that one must observe and recognize between the hood and very well to do neighborhoods and schools and wonder why does the hood consistently house freed African-American(minorities) as a majority and the more affluent neighborhoods always seem to house more White, Indian and Asians with very few freed African-Americans(minorities)?

However, the mind of many freed African-American(minorities) are still not free due to the prison of generational ignorance that prohibits this segment of the population from culturally integrating or appreciating the deliverance of the rainbow of thought to freedom. However, in 2011, the freedom of thought is enjoyed by most progressive freed African-American(minorities) who are educated of all the rights and benefits the law provides to freed African-Americans (minorities) today.

This includes well to do freed African-American (minority) entrepreneurs that have taken advantage of what Malcolm X, Dr. Martin L. King Jr. and the civil rights movement exemplified in the song, "we shall overcome". I hope all freed African-American (minorities) will get the message 299 hundred years later after the discontinued doctrine of Willie Lynch in America and will join us, better late than never.

Chapter 3

Marriage/Divorce today with kids involved, "The Internal mist."

I always ask people what is kindness and sweetness in your relationship and how did you get it so good with each other? Some would reply that they had to grow and learn from each other and many would point out challenging circumstances that promoted their relationships from a Christian faith principle to dating while enhancing the sanctity of the marriage itself.

I have to keep it real with the integrity of where I am coming from and that is my reality of my former marriage that I experienced in my own life. If you the reader read my book, "Invasion of the Baby Daddy" you would be aware of the drama that fictional story based on real life experienced caused for days in the book.

However, that made things into a great story of real life events and eventually even great reading of what to stay away from in domestic situations that involved baby mommas and baby daddies when the law conjoins biological parents together at the hip.

Unfortunately, the innocent bi-standing marital individual is powerless over the joint legal status law that over rules your marriage vows or your love as a man or woman, in love with the internal mist of these situations.

What happens when two people hook up despite of the outcome of the joint legal status laws in one state and try to defy the stain of intrusion by an opposing parent into the very lives of one mom or dad that is dying inside after the turning over of a child to a Biological parent based on a court order? Furthermore, the outcome of this obvious tragedy was done to have a life with the spouse, chosen to move out of the state, from a chaotic situation.(scenario from the book, "Invasion of the Baby Daddy".)

Meanwhile, the life of childless parenthood tears at the heart of that mom or the dad. How can one deal with this burden of often feeling guilty or walking away from one child and sometimes feeling like they made a mistake or a bad decision after the fact?

This phenomenon is called the Internal Mist and believe me it is very real and it happens more in America than most people can even imagine especially in the lives of African-Americans today.

To begin to talk about this subject you must take the characters from the book, Invasion of the Baby Daddy" and apply them appropriately in this situation. Dr. Mark Sand and Rachel Sand meet at the airport and decided to try to make their lives work out in the ending story line of the book, Invasion of the Baby Daddy.

Consequently, none of them are aware of the tactics that the Baby Daddy would use to yet antagonize Rachel with the cries of her son that was now with the father living out of state. Rachel desperately wanted her child to be turned over to her by calling the bluff of the father and allowing him to feel the pressure to raise his child under the penalty that Rachel brought upon herself by perjuring herself.

Additionally, being in contempt of court with false testimony and breaking the court order previously provided with the judges rule in the state of Georgia.

The plot thickens now that Rachel and Dr. Mark Sand now have a child of their own that is only two weeks old. Dr. Mark Sand is happy and asks Rachel, "Hey baby are you now going to stay here with me and keep the baby here and enjoy the house that I have built for you and the family?

Rachel responds yes baby, I will stay with you however Rachel did not totally disclose that she had already made provisions to return back to her living quarters where she yet had her job and unfinished business in Georgia.

Dr. Mark Sand loved his child and would never abandon her; however, after two weeks of the baby girl being born in Texas, Rachel is returning back to her former life in Georgia with Dr. Mark Sand's little two week old baby.

I cannot tell you the pain of that event when a man who loves a child, has to lose it because of nothing he did; but, due to some bitch ass situation that has nothing to do with him at all or his new born child. Let me disclose first hand that this is a heart wrenching thing that I would not wish on anyone who truly loved their child. So the situation is that the new Dad, Dr. Mark Sand has to come to grips with losing his new born child due to the joint legal status that surrounded another man's child; unfortunately, from a court order that Dr. Mark Sand did not know anything about when he married Rachel.

To add insult to injury, Rachel his wife is yet leaving with the new born two week old baby to be with her son from a previous relationship. Rachel is feeling torn between sharing a life with Dr. Mark Sand her husband or keeping the two kids and holding down a job by herself. The older child is spoiled and often difficult to control from a different Dad that now has joint legal status over his child that now cannot leave the state of Georgia. Rachel is contemplating to stay or to leave the state to live with Dr. Mark Sand her husband.

This is what I call the Internal Mist Syndrome because this situation is full of drama and turmoil for all involved especially the newly married individual who is helpless to the law and the deception of a marriage.

All marriages were meant to last forever but this situation has torn holes in it due to adding this devastating circumstance. The Internal mist is so common in the African-American community because of the way we live our lives by sexual satisfaction but with little responsibility attached to our actions in life. Most uneducated African-Americans have children very early in life without proper planning for life in the future.

This phenomenon can have devastating consequences especially when you add additional children within a new relationship or marriage win the challenges of the past life of another man's child is not properly organized for a peaceful future.

Dr. Mark Sand filed for divorce and did it not to get rid of his marriage per se out of rage or anger at Rachel. He applied for divorce after seeing Rachel's heart torn over many weeks that turned into months of lonely time without his child and worst without a life he had planned for.

Moreover, if Rachel could not come with him and live with the court order that was rendered, allowing her child to be raised with the biological father. Rachel was advised by Dr. Sand that with both children, she could stay in Georgia if she could not live with the court order.

Besides legally, Dr. Sand could be held liable by law to pay another man's child support even if the child is not his simply because Rachel would be his dependent as well as her court appointed debt. Rachel would have to provide child support for her child if she left her job and moved with Dr. Sand as the court ordered her to pay child support.

Meanwhile, Rachel has a streak of bad circumstances. One day Rachel, starts her car outside her home in Georgia against wise advice that Dr. Mark Sand had previously given her over the years. All of a sudden some thug Negro jumped in the car as the doors were not locked and drove away with Rachel's car.

Rachel is frantic and hears the fear move her insides as she calls Dr. Mark Sand to tell him what has just happened, "Mark, I just got my car stolen" said, Rachel.

Dr. Mark Sand, replied Rachel how did this happen and please tell me the truth?"

Rachel said, "I don't want to tell you because I know you are going to get mad at me."

Dr. Mark Sand replied, 'what are you talking about Rachel, you are not making any sense right now, what happened to our baby is everybody alright?"

Rachel sighed for a moment and replied, "Alright, Mark here is what happened today, I left the car running in the drive way and someone took the car and drove off with it. The baby was with me and she is alright and I am okay but the care is gone!"

"What!" said Dr. Mark Sand, "what do you mean the car is gone, didn't I tell you not to keep the damn car running while you went into the house, Rachel did you call the police already to report this car theft!"

Rachel began to cry and said, "I knew I should not have told you I knew you would make me feel like this and I already feel bad enough right now Mark, damn!"

"Alright! Alright, well what are you going to do now? You got the baby down there making me feel crazy right now and what about you considering coming here?" Dr. Mark Sand replied.

Rachel thought a second and said, "I am so torn with everything Mark everything is continuously happening to me and it is just getting tougher and tougher here now. Rachel continued, "I know my son will need his Dad but I know we can have a good thing too. I know that I have raised him all his life and I am his Mom and I will greatly miss him with all my heart Mark."

Dr. Mark Sand responded, "Rachel, I know this is hard on you and you have been gone for at least 2 months already with our little baby and I am wondering if you can ever come back here to Texas." Dr. Mark Sand continued, "Look Rachel, I know what I am going to tell you is hard but if you know it is not in your heart to come back here then let's just be divorced and I will come and see my baby and you can still keep the kids and we will just let life be as it is right now."

Rachel began to sob and Dr. Mark Sand felt his heart breaking just hearing her cry. It always broke him to the core to hear Rachel cry as if her heart was being ripped from within her in this paralyzing situation. However, he knew that at this moment that Rachel had to make a choice either to stay in Georgia or move with him to Texas. It was then that life for Dr. Mark Sand would change forever because Rachel looked at her life and told Dr. Mark Sand that she would come to live with him in Texas.

Dr. Mark Sand said, "Do you really mean it Rachel? If you really can't do it Rachel don't play with my heart, I will understand, I know this is hard for you. Dr. Mark

Sand continued, "I know that our baby will be alright and we can just let things be as they are and you do not have to put yourself through anymore pain from your decisions in your life."

Rachel replied, "Well Mark, my life here is just fading away and I can see where my son is spending more time with his dad and he is really enjoying it and I know his dad want hurt him and I know he will need a man in his life." Rachel Continued, "I want my life with you and I am so sorry for putting you through all this back and forth but this is my son Mark, he is my child just like our baby now is your child, Mark!"

Dr. Mark Sand replied, "I know that's why I am telling you Rachel if you cannot come to live with me and follow the court order then stay in Georgia. I know I want to live with my baby so badly but I do not want you to go through anymore regrets in your life. And I know that I am losing my time anyway with you and my baby I have not seen my baby in almost two month now. I mean this situation has already robbed me of the pregnancy of my first born child. Rachel, you spent all 9 months in Georgia and I could not even be with you for lama's classes or anything that a real father would feel with a wife and expecting his child!"

Rachel responded with anger, "Mark, don't you remember when you said that you did not think that my body would even have kids after the ectopic pregnancy and we loss that baby and I almost died Mark! Don't try to deny that you said that you doubted I would even have kids Mark and that hurt me but I refused to believe that Mark!" Rachel continued, "Mark you even ordered a paternity test the day the baby was born. Did you doubt the baby was yours? I also love my first child as any mother would!" I know you love our baby but I know that you do not want my son like you want our baby because you feel that he is a part of his dad's problems that led to the terrible situation that you have been dragged into Mark and I am sorry that you feel like that!"

Dr. Mark Sand replied, "Rachel I feel that your child is innocent and he is but, the court order is the thing that you or I cannot get around here and we have to be honest with that Rachel!" "You also have to understand that it is that damn court order that is keeping me away from my innocent child too!" Dr. Mark Sand continued, "That shit is killing me because all this shit happened before we were even married. Yet, I am suffering for what you and some stupid ass irresponsible baby daddy got going on that is stopping me from enjoying my life right now, do you understand that Rachel!"

Rachel began to cry and said to Dr. Mark Sand, "I know I messed up Mark damn, you do not have to keep reminding me of my mistakes in life and I know I have hurt you but I never meant for any of this to happen the way it did Mark! I do want to come up there and I will in the next few weeks. I promise, I just want to make sure that my child is alright with everything alright Mark, but I want you to know that I love you."

Dr. Mark Sand replied, "I love you too Rachel with all my heart, I just don't want to be in this situation all of my life, missing my baby and tearing our hearts away from each other with all this uncertainty all the damn time in our lives."

Finally, the few weeks passed, Rachel had made the call and finally came to Texas to live with Dr. Mark Sand, it had been almost two and half months since Dr. Mark Sand had seen his little new born baby that was almost two and half months old now. The first few weeks were great, Rachel and Dr. Mark Sand really tried to be around each other quite a bit and spent time making love and enjoying seeing the baby every day.

Dr. Mark Sand felt his world was finally complete and that all would be well. One day Rachel mentioned that she was tired of sitting in the house watching the baby all day while Dr. Mark Sand was out seeing his patients. Rachel stated to Dr. Mark Sands, "I am in this house all day Mark and it gets boring being here all day with just the baby and me. I mean if I want to be by myself all the time I could have had that type of life when I was in Georgia what so different with my life here Mark?"

Rachel continued, "I mean you are at work all day on your work days. I was a working woman when you met me, I was a working independent type of woman and I feel like I am losing myself with no job and just sitting here all day with the baby in this over 5,000 square foot home in Texas."

Dr. Mark Sand, felt confused and hurt by Rachel's statement he replied, "Rachel, what the hell are you started to complain about, you do not have to work at all being here and you knew you were not going to be working right away when you moved here with our little baby right now anyway!" Dr. Mark Sand continued, "Our baby is so small and now being a mother is what she needs, you do not have to run all around here like you did in Georgia that what is different. I come home every night Rachel and I am working as a Physician to take care of you and our baby. I am taking care of this mortgage and your mortgage in Georgia and I am not complaining about it at all. What is your big problem with making a life her with me when I am trying my damn best to give you a good life?"

Rachel held the baby and responded, "Mark, you do not appreciate anything that I have given up do you?"

"What, I know what you have given up Rachel, what are you talking about that's why I am working so hard to give you a good life here Rachel!" replied Dr. Mark Sand.

Rachel turned to Dr. Mark Sand saying, "I have given my son to his father and I have left my damn job and all I do now is just sit in this house and take care of our baby all day. I am not a sit at home all day kind of woman Mark!" Rachel continued, "I have made many sacrifices and you still work and go and I don't have anything to show for what I have done Mark and you just want your baby and don't care anything about what I have sacrificed so you can raise your baby Mark!"

Dr. Mark Sand replied, "Rachel, I told you before you moved up here that if you could not live with the decision to abide by the court order then to stay in Georgia. I knew you would miss your son but I have been paying for rental cars and plane tickets so you can see your son when you wanted to go to Georgia and you had already been home not even three weeks ago. Dr. Mark Sand continued, "Rachel I do appreciate all that you have done to be here and I am taking care of you but I still have to work and I can't be here on my work time Rachel, is it that you are just simply missing your son?"

"Why are you making this a separate issue the makes us fight and argue over these types of matters?" Rachel grabbed a photo of her and Dr. Mark Sand, Rachel shouted, "Mark, why did you want me to be here when you are working all the time and I am simply in the house with no friends or family around and I am not enjoying this every day in this house and taking care of the baby all the time stuff."

Rachel continued, "You have your work Mark and you can get out and you still can have the ability to have your friends and do things that you want to do." I am simply not thinking that you know what I have lost Mark and I am thinking I made am mistake by coming up here Mark!"

Rachel then grabs the wedding photo in a glass frame with yellow metal trimmings and opens the front French doors and threatens to throw the photo out the door onto to the porch and lawn of the house.

Dr. Mark Sand shouts, "Rachel what are you doing? Close the door and put that photo back on the table! Rachel I do not know what is into you tonight but I am doing everything that I said I would do to make our lives work here and to hear you talk like this is sad to me. I thought we were going to make our lives work at this point especially with our baby her now; close the door Rachel, don't throw that picture out there, put the damn picture down!"

Dr. Mark Sand continued, "You know that is my favorite photo because it reminds me when we were happy before all this shit Rachel that has robbed us of our life together, we used to have such a great time and now all we do is fight and argue with each other Rachel. It seems all you want to do is argue what do you want from me? You are now getting destructive and acting like a crazy woman trying to destroy what we have together in this house that is nice stuff. Why do you want to destroy that photo and get all destructive in this house Rachel?"

Rachel held the baby in one hand and the photo in another and opened the door further and shouted, "Mark, you are not the one that has given up a job and a child and all I have to show for what I have done is to just be here in this house all day with a baby!" Rachel then lifted the photo and threw it toward the concrete steps and side walk and the manicured lawn design.

Dr. Mark Sand, yelled, "No Rachel stop!" However, by then the photo was in flight and Dr. Mark Sand ran toward the front door and Rachel walked away hurriedly with the baby in hand as if nothing mattered to her. Rachel was feeling angry and shouted, "If you want this fucking picture so bad then you go and get it!" As

Dr. Mark Sand ran toward the door the photo took off from Rachel's hand and immediately the photo crashed to the cement and the glass frame shattered squish!! The sound was incredible and seemingly tore through the soul of Dr. Mark Sand as the frame burst into splintered pieces on the side walk and in the lawn itself. This incident happened at night in the still of the night in an upscale vintage neighborhood that was quiet and safe until this angry rage tore the calm of silence by the echoing sound of shattering glass and tearing souls at the same time in one defining moment in time.

Dr. Mark Sand felt in his heart that he would never be the same again and the trust and devotion he once had for Rachel toward a great marital life seemingly began to unravel right before him. Dr. Mark Sand went out to pick up the glass with a flash light and the porch light to ensure no neighbors saw broken glass or even heard the domestic disturbance of the only African-American couple on this street in this affluent neighborhood. The photo was destroyed scarred and torn and ripped with the broken glass and shattered frame.

Dr. Mark Sand came back into the house and went into the media room which was upstairs and Rachel was there yet was angry and yelled, "You don't appreciate what I did Mark and that's why I did what I did with that Photo, I don't even know why I even came here anymore, I am not happy here as I thought I would be Mark!" Rachel Continued, "When you do come home you only watch CNN on the TV and you may come to bed sometime, you seem to work in your office every night and it seems that you only come to bed at 2:00 or 3:00 o'clock in the damn morning. I know you do a lot of your work on computer but I feel I am just here by myself Mark and I can't stand it Mark! I know you wanted to give me a good life and a nice house and you work hard but I want a life too and I am not having the life I want here Mark. I want to be making my own money and doing my own thing like you do every day!"

Dr. Mark Sand, replied, "you know Rachel, you got some fucking nerve throwing shit out of this house in this nice neighborhood, you are getting destructive and talking crazy and you are always threatening to leave and taking my baby away from here trying to hurt me like your baby daddy hurt you. You are doing the same shit he did to you and you can't even see that!"

Dr. Mark Sand continued, "Rachel, how the hell do you think that I am able to pay your mortgage and my mortgage if I do not work, Yes, I watch CNN a lot because I like the fucking news but I am working all day, can't a man come home and watch the news in peace and have a good meal?"

Dr. Mark Sand continued, "You know I work at night because I am a college Professor or have you forgotten about that as well Rachel? You are so fucking selfish and into yourself you don't see what I am doing without one complaint at all! Rachel you have access to my car when I get home. If you did not leave your car running outside like a damn fool, you would have a car right now and that nigger would have never stole it in the first place, Rachel!" shouted Dr. Mark Sand.

Rachel replied, "Uh huh, you see there you are throwing that damn shit in my face again, Mark! That could have happened to anyone and you know it! I am always being made to feel stupid and you are always talking down at me and I am tired of that shit!"

Dr. Mark Sand went to lay the baby down in her crib because the baby was sleeping and closed the bedroom door not to wake the baby. Dr. Mark Sand went into his office to get away from all the frustration.

Rachel followed him and began her rants all over again. Rachel shouted, "you see I knew your ass was going to go into this office and not talk to me!"

Dr. Mark Sand replied, "Rachel, what the hell is there to talk about! I mean I miss out on almost three months of my baby's life including the pregnancy and you have been here now for only almost 2 months and you are frustrated talking about you hate that you came here. It hurts me that you are not happy and regret being here when I am working my ass off to keep everything going for us Rachel!"

Dr. Mark Sand continues, "You are getting destructive and you broke that photo and I cannot believe that you would even do something like that Rachel! What could you possibly want to discuss at this point Rachel?" Rachel grabs Dr. Mark Sands and punches him in his lower chin and upper chest, thump goes the sound!

Dr. Mark Sand and is trying to shield his face and warns Rachel not to grab at his neck and to stop trying to hit him because she was getting close to his necklace of pure gold that has been on his neck for over 19 years that Dr. Mark Sand has had around his neck since the first gulf war in 1991. Suddenly, the worst fear happened Dr. Mark Sand felt a strong scratch on his neck and a pull that would be the break of his gold necklace and this would be the second destructive thing that Dr. Mark Sand experienced in this one evening with Rachel.

At this moment of reality Dr. Mark Sand grabbed Rachel and pushed her away from him and noticed his gold necklace was off his neck and fell in his hands.

Dr. Mark Sands never laid a hand on Rachel but shoved her away and shouted, "Rachel you have broken this photo and you have now gotten so destructive to even hit at me and now have even broken my 19 year old necklace that has never been off my neck before! I do not want to see you tonight just stay the fuck away from me! If you want to become destructive and you think I am so boring and you don't want to be here with me and appreciate the life I am trying to give us then I don't want your ass here!"

Dr. Mark Sand continued angrily, "If you ever break anything in this house again then your ass will be gone from my house!"

Dr. Mark Sand realized that his anger was at its peak and went into the guess quarters of the house and felt tears come to his eyes as he slammed the door and fell into the guess bed and cried out of pure frustration and pain within.

It was evident that his heart was changing and what he felt for Rachel was not registering in his heart anymore. He battled inside do I stay here to keep my baby and be in misery or do I just let Rachel and the baby leave and be a type of father that I never wanted to be in my life? Dr. Mark Sand never wanted to see his life come down to this type of choice in life but he knew that fighting and arguing and watching his actual life die before him trying to live with Rachel and raise his child was beginning to not become the reality that he anticipated. Sadly, Rachel was already planning to take off again and go back home for the summer and take the baby again with her.

This is the Internal Mist syndrome where men and women have to decide on the future of a dying relationship because of the love of their children even though the love for the spouse or lover has already died over continuing fights and arguments. It is the arena where couples feel so distant from each other that even in a 5,000 sq ft home the environment is so toxic that the house itself feels about 100sq ft and the very sight of the person with that negative energy is toxic to your spirit and its sad that many couples walk on egg shells to try to not piss each other off at these times in relationships.

Rachel leaves 2 days later for another 7 week period to her home. Therefore, the baby has been gone for all that time and Dr. Mark Sand is feeling distant from Rachel but is missing his baby terribly. He makes a phone call to Rachel to inquire about his child and Rachel yells at him and says, "The baby is fine and we are enjoying our time away from you!" Rachel continued, 'Mark, you don't want us anyway, I don't know why you acted like you wanted me and the baby to be there with you? You don't need us; I don't want to be with someone who I have to fight with just to have a life with all the damn time, Mark! I am here with my son and I can see that he needs and misses his momma. I will call you later and talk to you later, by!"

"Rachel! Rachel! God damn why are you acting like this, I am missing my baby and all I can do is work with you to try to see my baby as you know I am a father!" The phone goes silent and Dr. Mark Sand is furious and understands that he is in a real mess and begins to understand that divorce sounds better even though he knows that he will more than likely loose his baby. He knew this would result on seeing his baby on weekends, holidays and in 3 weeks the summer months according to the divorce decree.

Divorce ultimately hurts the heart of any true father or mother that has to decide to leave a toxic relationship that will also divide the parent from the child in the process. However, staying in a toxic relationship where arguing and domestic violence are the daily events in the relationship cause harm not only to the family structure including parents but worst even the children as well. Unfortunately, when children have to grow up seeing this toxicity they can often absorb this and blame themselves as if they are the cause of the two parents fighting. Moreover, the children are always innocent of any parental divisions.

Dr. Mark Sand began to look for a family counselor with divorce and marriage experience from a Christian and God fearing basis that will help guide Dr. Mark Sand and Rachel as a last resort toward redemption if it could be found in their relationship and with time even lead to remarriage.

The counselor was found and he was a Bishop and a great authority of marriage and family counseling and family affairs counseling. He was an African-American counselor that made Dr. Mark Sand felt great and presented commonality with the Bishop and an allegiance toward helping to resolve this paralyzing situation.

Rachel returned with the baby a week later and agreed to go to counseling with Dr. Mark Sand and met with the Bishop. Considerably, the Bishop was very warm and approachable toward both Dr. Mark Sand and Rachel and demonstrated no bias at all. Instead, the Bishop listened and was very direct and honest with both Dr. Mark Sand and Rachel.

The Bishop asked Rachel, "Rachel, what do you feel that you have gained since you are now with Dr. Mark Sand and you two are together now and do you feel you regret your decision to come here to live to make your family work?"

Rachel replied, "well, I feel since I have been here that Mark has not provided me with everything that I thought we would have, like marrying me as he had talked about before I moved here and I feel that I sacrificed my son and my job for an unrealistic relationship in my opinion and I have personal regrets right now."

The Bishop asked, "Rachel wasn't it the courts that ordered you to turn over your son to the biological father if you left Georgia so that decision was not made be you?"

"Yes", replied Rachel.

The Bishop responded softly, "well you see that the court made that decision about your son for you and nothing was made by you at all. The was a decision that was already predetermined and with you making a choice of where your heart was the court did the rest not you directly doing anything but following your heart and that is honorable."

The Bishop pointed his attention towards Dr. Mark Sand and asked, "Mark your former wife seems to want to remarry you and stated that you made it clear that you would remarry her once she came to live with you and establish a family life with you. What is your hesitation of that and where is the problem in remarrying Rachel at this point?"

Dr. Mark Sand sits back and sighed with a breath and responded, "Well Bishop it seems that my plans to remarry Rachel were based on what I predicted would be happy with us coming together and really enjoying each other. So far Rachel and I have not been together for more than a few weeks consecutively sense she has been here and Rachel continues to threaten to leave and return to her home in Georgia every time we have a disagreement. Rachel and I have been arguing and at each other's throat every day. Honestly, thinking about remarrying her is the farthest thing from my mind right now and that's why we came here to seek help if there is something we can do to change the course of where we are currently heading."

The Bishop sat back and shook his head saying, "you two are really good people and it seems that you two at least care for each other. You have this beautiful baby here between the two of you and you are here together to try to work things out. But I also see that there is some mistrust and past hurt emotions here that seemingly were never truly dealt with properly in your lives. I see that Mark you don't trust Rachel and Rachel I see that you do not totally trust in Mark anymore. According to Mark, he does not trust you Rachel because he blames you now for all the court orders that you never shared with him before marriage. This also includes never totally disclosing to Mark about the secret lies when you perjured yourself on the witness stand in your trial against your child's father that you lost because you lied under oath and forever put a stain on the marriage you once had."

The Bishop continued, "Mark, it seems that Rachel is not trusting in your word that you said that you would remarry her and make her life feel that her sacrifices will be for some valid reason and not just simply dangling in the wind of life waiting on you to make good on your word without giving Rachel some guarantees that she will have a life with you and a family that she once trusted she would have with you for this baby and her son."

The Bishop removed his glasses and glanced at Rachel and Dr. Mark Sand and evaluated for a moment his next series of moves were in silence, then he spoke these words. "I have seen so many couples come through this office and many have some small problems and some have some very challenging cuts in the marriage that can forever damage one's life. You two have a situation I like to call the Internal mist. This situation you are in is called this because you have two people that are no longer in love with the sanctity of a healthy relationship. In this situation two people are holding on to the vapors of what used to be a great thing in hopes that the substance of what was can be again. The problem with the Internal mist syndrome is that there is usually nothing left for the two people to hang onto because everything is dissolved or gone that was once solid and tangible in the relationship, all that remains is the mist of a lack of commitment, the mist of broken promises and finally the mist of something that was once joyful and fulfilling is merely two people with children wasting their lives even living together but there is no trust of life at all.

The Bishop continued, "I am sure that the two of you love your baby here very much but if you can not love each other with commitment and devotion toward each other to work together in your lives then the Internal mist syndrome will be your fate and you simply should cut your losses now and go on with your lives. You both will disappoint each other living with the mind you have now. I have been a certified family and marriage counselor for almost 32 years and I have been married for 36 years and I have seen couples come and sadly I have watched many couples detach and fall away from their marriage.

"I want you both to know that there are no perfect marriages and Hollywood is just what it is fake, make believe and even worst unrealistic. A relationship without commitment and trust is the same way, unbelievable not sustainable and unrealistic with just the internal mist of what the solid foundation used to be of the former relationship. In my opinion, it is not good trying to hang on to a dying relationship solely for the kids."

The bishop continued, "Honestly, at the end of the day, the children will grow up seeing two parents disliking each other and this could hurt the children and typically kids absorb this divided emotional disruption and can even blame themselves that you all the parents can not make it work out. However, usually in the Internal Mist the child is really the only thing at this point that you both probably love without hesitation; in this syndrome that's not the problem it's the love that you both once had that is now gone and the real question is, what are both of you going to do to rationally and purposely get that good thing back?" "If you both are not at the point that you can commit yourself toward a unity of life as one together with trust, love and God as the head of your union then cut your losses and end this effort now before you waste more of your time and hurt each other more for doing something that's not in your heart to do at all. I have been around a long time and I know how to be honest with you and how to not make decisions for you but to let you know if you're going in the right direction or even in the wrong direction seeking a worthwhile goal."

The Bishop looked at Dr. Mark Sand and Rachel as he sat back in his chair and looked over his thin framed glasses as if he knew what he had said was already hitting home for Dr. Mark Sand and Rachel. The Bishop offered to pray and grabbed Dr. Mark Sand and Rachel's hand and asked them to bow their heads.

Bishop lead them in prayer and gave them a home work assignment in which he stated, "Alright Mark and Rachel, this is something that if you want your good thing back you really have to get to know each other again. "

The Bishop continued, "One problem I heard from both of you is that you both never knew each other well enough to be married in the first place. Rachel, you living here and Mark you living there that's no way to get to know anyone and you cannot become familiar with each other over the phone or by email. You must have a personal daily commitment of dating and getting to know each other over a period of time together before marriage not after. If you do not have this period of time together, then you are truly building your life together on sinking sand. Moreover, you will never really know who you have married. Rachel and Mark unfortunately, this is exactly what happen to the two of you. Obviously, you both of course are good people but you never got a real chance to get to know each other; that would include things like your habits, fears and baby daddy issues that Rachel had. Naturally, even the laid back professional life that you want Mark was not totally understood because you two did not have the proper time and life before marriage to get to know each other. This turmoil of the Internal Mist you're going through was not supposed to be experienced now after marriage, divorce and now an innocent child between you two. What you are experiencing now was supposed to be found out before the marriage, divorce or the children by the time you are taking things to this point. If you truly want to give yourselves a real shot at life for remarriage you must get to know each other very well and basically start all over with each other again. Remember don't bring up the past and let go of yesterdays pain, do not speak hurtful words to each other."

The Bishop continued, "Mark take Rachel on a date without your baby for an evening or weekend and just laugh and talk and do things like a new couple would and see if you two can truly find the passion of what your lives together once was. I truly hope that there is not just internal mist between the inner souls of the two of you. That is the end of our session today, I will keep you both in prayer and I will see you in two weeks from today."

Rachel and Mark left the Bishop's office and had for the first time realized that they had to really try to make their lives work.

Rachel really tried to not argue with Mark and Mark tried not to argue with Rachel. It seemed that the words of the Bishop and his own life experience with biblical views on marriage really hit to the heart of Rachel and Mark.

A few weeks passed and Rachel and Mark began to try to do much better and not sweat the small stuff. Small arguments would erupt here and there but it always seem to be a real trial for Rachel and Mark to totally unite and communicate with each other without lashing out with comments about Mark's life, family and long hours at work from Rachel.

Furthermore, this would escalate towards Rachel's mistake with her court issues and baby daddy issues that ruined their marriage from Mark.

Along with the small rants the love making would commence and sex was always good with Rachel and Mark, however, their new life together was not a real great experience for them and trying not to argue or make each other upset was like changing a hot light bulb with your bare hands hoping not to be burned.

It seemed that the words of the Bishop's Internal Mist may have some kind of truth to them; this really began to weigh heavily on the mind of Dr. Mark Sand and Rachel alike. Rachel and Dr. Mark Sand would try to make love and say nice things to each other. They never went out on that date with each other without their child because they had trouble finding a babysitter and no family lived nearby.

Rachel even began to calm down on the complaining being home by herself as much and Dr. Mark Sand actually quit his university teaching job to be home more with Rachel and their baby. Usually, when Dr. Mark Sand came home he began to give Rachel a break from being with the baby where she could take the car and go to the movies even run errands.

It seemed that life was beginning to mellow out and for a first time since living together Rachel and Dr. Mark

Sand appeared to be happy with each other even laughing more with each other.

However, it seems the Devil himself knew how to disturb the happiness and that was with the baby daddy calling and disturbing Rachel over her son's ability to talk with her and the baby daddy seemed to stand in the way of Rachel communicating with her son. This would place Rachel in a very agitated mode and bring up anger issues that would be acted out against Dr. Mark Sand.

Rachel would get so upset that when it came to Dr. Mark Sand she would go outside and avoid talking to him. This allowed Rachel's anger to build in her and finally erupt with the physical violence and verbal agitation that Dr. Mark Sand would become a victim of in life that he could not control or change.

Adversely, it involved a situation that was outside of his grasp as a man, to protect Rachel. The unfortunate reality is that Dr. Mark Sand knew that he would never totally heal Rachel of the stain in her life from the experience with this baby daddy figure; that was allowed to legally invade Rachel's life.

The Internal Mist flamed up in this sense and reminded both Dr. Mark Sand and Rachel that their divorce was real and could remain of their torn relationship. Ironically, this reminded them of the mistrust and devastation of the divorce that caused so much drama and discourse in the life as they were trying to rebuild with one another with counseling.

The two weeks had passed; Dr. Mark Sand and Rachel went back to the Bishop at his office. The Bishop observed them both and stated, "So did you all use the homework assignments that I had given you?"

Dr. Mark Sand replied, "Uh, yes we have been trying to do better with what you have given us since the first session with you Bishop, I actually quit at the University to be home more with the family and I give Rachel the car when I get home so she can have a break from the baby. So I feel I am really trying on my part."

Bishop asked Rachel, "Okay, Rachel what is it that you have improved on since we last got together in our counseling session?"

Rachel, sat back and stated, I have tried to not argue as much with Mark and tried not to fight over the small stuff too much anymore. I am trying to relax at home and make the house more enjoyable with the family and cook more instead of not making life better with Mark and complaining as much. I still have some things to clear out but I am trying to get better."

"So have you all had a chance to get to know each other without any harsh words or fighting or arguing toward negative impacting emotions as before you both came here?" asked the Bishop.

Dr. Mark Sand replied, "Well Bishop, I try to not argue with Rachel and I also try to stay out of her way when she is angry. I try not to press her buttons but I know there are things that I cannot control with her and the negative feedback of her life with her baby daddy often can be a bit much. I am the one that gets the emotional attacks that the man who caused this mess does not get."

"Well, Bishop, Mark is always throwing in my face my past and sometimes it bothers me and I always feel like he is putting me down all the time. Even when I am trying to get over the fact that my child and my job is not a part of my life every day. I feel Mark has a problem appreciating what I did to be here with him. It is not easy and I know Mark has been good to me and yes I do have some fault in how our life has been affected but no one is perfect and Mark makes me feel like I am nothing sometimes," said Rachel.

The Bishop said, "Well, are you more focused on where you want to be as a family and as far as what you want for each other in your life?" Rachel said, I do love Mark and I feel I have already proven that by what I have done to be here with him and I know that I want my family with Mark, I just want us to work well with each other and be appreciated for who I am as someone who is willing to be a part of life with Mark."

The Bishop interjected, "Rachel have you got over the sacrifice of being with Mark and have you made up in your mind that this was a move that you made out of commitment for a life with Mark as someone you love and need and can't live without in your life?"

Rachel replied, "I have seen that my move here is one that I have made to make a life with Mark and we are not where I thought we would be but I know that I do love Mark and now I just want a life where I can feel fulfilled in my career life just as Mark does and I am not experiencing that. I am an independent woman and I like being able to have my own money, job and take care of the kids and have something of my own."

Bishop interjected, "Rachel and Mark as I have stated to both of you in my last session, it takes 2 people to become one in a marriage and commit toward love and life with each other. This means that the two of you must be going in the same direction to make anything between you work well for a future together. I am praying that the two of you will see the potential of being equally yoked and as one in a relationship towards each other.

As I mentioned if you continue to think divided and cannot commit then cut your losses now and let the chips fall where they may. But if you can make this work then you have to become one and that is not at the altar that is during the engagement and the time that love is in your heart toward the alter not after you have said I do and then try to find your commitment of each other. That is a disaster and will never last because love and commitment did not lead you to the alter in the first place. If you are not committed in love before marriage then the marriage itself will never even have a leg to stand on. Unfortunately, to add a child to this mess is what is happening in our society today, the internal mist syndrome of America."

The Bishop asked, "Mark have you ever told Rachel that you loved her?

Mark replied, "Yes I have told her before and I do love Rachel.

The Bishop interjected, "Mark look at Rachel and tell her that.

Mark turn in his chair to Rachel and said, "Rachel, I do love you and I love our baby and I have tried to make a happy home for you to raise our family in. I know I am not exciting all the time but I am always trying to build our family life to be good for us and I want us to work I just don't want to be a victim of your past when you get mad but I do love you very much."

The Bishop stated, "Rachel tell Mark why you love him and what you want from him."

Rachel turned her chair to Mark and said, "Mark, you know I love you and I know we have had our moments but I want you to know that I do love you and I want you to be a part of my life and have a family with you. I feel we can make it and be a great couple as we did before everything went wrong with us. I know I am not perfect but I am trying Mark to make things right for us and I know I have my anger moments but I am trying to get better Mark. But you must admit sometimes you do make me feel like I am not appreciated and I think you can work on that."

"Well now, I am glad that you both at least seem a little more focused in this session with these acknowledgements to each other. You just have to now begin to continue to get to know each other more. You two are not quite committed enough for remarriage but at least we are better at getting our priorities on track on what you two would lose if you truly lost each other. Don't let the internal mist syndrome of nothingness win over your minds and you end up with nothing left between each other struggling over petty things that don't matter any way in the large scope of things to come in your life," said the Bishop.

"That's all for today and I will pray for the both of you and I feel God will show you both what his will is concerning your lives. Simply trust God and put your faith in him and as God did great things in my life with my children, he will do the same for both of you. I hope to see you both in two weeks. Let us pray. God show Mark and Rachel what your will is in their lives and lead them and protect their child and keep your guidance of wisdom with them and allow them to know you as their God so whatever your will is in their lives that Lord they can humble themselves to that direction for their lives. Lord you know their hearts reveal to them your purpose for their lives as a family in your son Jesus name, Amen." said the Bishop.

Dr. Mark Sand and Rachel left out of the Bishop's office and as they picked up the baby Dr. Mark Sand and Rachel held hands and walked to the car. It was if things were heading in the right direction.

Rachel and Dr. Mark Sand seemed happy and all seemed to be going well for about a week after leaving the Bishop's office and experiencing his wonderful prayer for their lives.

A week after leaving the Bishop's office Dr, Mark Sand was returning home from work and heard some shouting and screaming in the kitchen area that was adjacent to the garage entry way. It was Rachel on the phone again arguing with her baby daddy. The night before Dr. Mark Sand came home and Rachel had threaten to change his child's name and actually physically tried to keep him from driving his car to make copies of her original birth certificate. It actually was crazy; Rachel snatched off Dr. Mark Sand's glasses and even tried to physically restrain him from leaving the house. Dr. Mark Sand had to physically pry his way to the door while Rachel was physically fighting to hold him back. Both Rachel and Dr. Mark Sand was careful not to hurt the baby in this commotion but it got ugly with physical grabbing and shouts and screams of anger from both Rachel and Dr. Mark Sand.

Dr. Mark Sand shouted, "Rachel are you crazy you are not going to change my child's name and take my child from me, I will never allow you to get away with that shit, I promise you that!

Rachel shouted, "I am going to tell our baby that you did not want her and I am going to change her name and let her know you are just a typical Black ass baby daddy! I am going to let our baby know that you do not want your family and you did not appreciate me for what I have done you for Mark! I left my job and allowed my damn child to go to his fucking baby daddy for you Mark!"

Dr. Mark Sand shouted, "What the hell is this shit! I have paid for Attorneys and your travel and all the getting your hair done and you're fucking rental cars and plane tickets for you and your son because your punk ass baby daddy does not want to pay for travel for his own damn child to even see you, Rachel! I have faithfully paid for your mortgage and my mortgage and I put money in your pocket to help you with your bills and take of care my child. I have not complained one time about any of it, all I have asked of you is to be sweet to me and show me some fucking respect. I have paid for counseling to help us get better and you snap after all that and now you want to change my baby's identity because you are mad at me over your baby daddy's bull shit again that you are still dealing with!"

Dr. Mark Sand continued, "I thought we said you were not going to let that ruin our life anymore with that old crap of that court order bullshit that actually ruined our marriage in the first place! I have already missed out on the pregnancy of my first child and I have even missed months of my baby's life since my baby has been born in the world because of your fucked up past life! Let me remind you, I have nothing to do with your past, but I have suffered in my life simply because I gave my heart to someone that was not responsible and a liar! Rachel you were not even ready for the life I offered you; that is my damn fault, I have to live with that. I see now remarriage is not even a rational thought with your lying ass!"

Dr. Mark Sand tried to leave the house through the side door with his baby's birth certificate and hospital records to make copies at a local copy store.

Rachel blocked the door way with her body and shouted, "You aint going nowhere Mark, I aint going nowhere and you aint going nowhere either!" Rachel continued, "You don't appreciate me and who I am and what I have done to be here Mark. You have made me feel terrible and now you just simply act all senseless like I don't mean anything to you! You are not leaving this house, and you are not leaving me, do you hear me Mark? I am not going to allow you to leave and I have custody of our child per the divorce so you will not be with her everyday if I go back to Georgia any way!"

The struggles was on and Dr. Mark Sand actually picked Rachel up and moved her out of his way, Dr. Mark sand cried out, "Ahh! get out of my way; you are not going to hold me hostage from leaving in my own house! Your ass is real crazy get out of my damn way, right now!"

Dr. Mark Sand never put a hand on Rachel violently or hit her. It was a scuffle to get through the door and finally Dr. Mark Sand got through the door into the garage.

Rachel Grabbed his glasses off his face and shouted, "Uh huh you can't leave if you can't see Mark I got your damn glasses so how far do you think you are going to get, Mark?"

"Ahh! Damn, give me my damn glasses Rachel stop this crazy shit right now, what the fuck do you think you are doing?"

Dr. Mark Sand got another pair of glasses from his house and placed his baby in the car with him.

Rachel shouted, "I am going too and you are not going to leave me!" Rachel got into the car and took the car keys out of the ignition.

"Ahh! You crazy ass woman what the hell are you doing?" Dr. Mark Sand continued, "put the key back in the ignition or give me my damn car keys Rachel right now!" I see you are taking shit way too far now and I am getting pissed off from this shit, really pissed! You threaten to change my baby's name and basically try to erase me from my child's life. I am not going to stand for this shit at all! As far as our plans for remarriage and counseling look at what it got us Rachel just look at us tonight!"

Dr. Mark Sand went back into the house and got the second car key set and got into the car and started the car with Rachel and the baby in it and proceeded to back out of the garage when the garage door opened.

Rachel opened the front passenger car door suddenly and Shouted, "I know you are not going to drive with the car door opened down the road, Mark!"

Dr. Mark Sand put the car in reverse from park determined to drive the vehicle to make copies to keep a copy of the originals to protect his child's identity. Rachel reached up to throw the car back in another gear and Dr. Mark sand shouted, "Wait! What the fuck are you doing God dam it! Don't you see I am driving?"

"You doing all this crazy shit Rachel and you can actually cause a fucking accident out here tonight!" Do you really want to hurt me and our child that fucking bad God dam it, you really that fucking crazy?"

Dr. Mark Sand continued, "You do not have to worry because I am going to give you the papers on our child and you do have custody. I am no longer afraid if you leave or where ever the hell your ass goes as long as my baby is okay your can do what the fuck you like , I don't give a fuck anymore Rachel! I have tried everything to help us with counseling, money for you, putting money in your bank account giving you the car when I get home everything and it is not ever enough for you! Well now I realize you are just a crazy angry violent woman that I do not want my child to see fighting with her father all the damn time! We are getting you a rental car and you are getting out of my house and I don't care where you go from here! I will just remain divorced from you and take care of my child according to the divorce court order!"

Finally, the car drove off and all arrived at the copy store and Dr. Mark Sand made copies of his child's birth certificate and proof of birth papers.

Thankfully, the ride back home was uneventful and Dr. Mark Sand gave Rachel the original copies of the baby's birth records.

At the house Dr. Mark Sand went to the guess room locked and closed the bed room door, prayed to God for clarity of the situation he was experiencing and to take his anger and frustration away and fell asleep.

Rachel knocked on the door and said, "Mark, can I talk to you about this tonight!"

With no answer from Dr. Mark Sand Rachel and the baby went into the master bed room suite and fell asleep also it was at least 2:15am.

Now, this is the next day that Dr. Mark Sand is returning from a day of work as he is driving up in the garage gets out of his car and hears Rachel and her baby daddy arguing once again over their child.

Dr. Mark Sand listens just for a moment because he did not want to once again become a victim of Rachel's violent rage of anger that was once again caused by the terrible relationship she had with her baby's daddy and their constant storm of antics over their child.

Rachel shouted at her baby daddy while on the phone, "dam it, let me speak to my child! God dam it let me speak to my son! You aint nothing but a no good example of a father and I hate dealing with your ass any way; put my God damn child on the fucking phone nigga! I don't want to talk to your ass, put my damn child on the fucking phone, right now!"

Finally, Rachel's son is allowed to talk on the phone by the baby daddy. "Hey baby, momma is here, I will see you soon and I will be coming down there very soon to see you okay. I can hear in your voice that you are sad and that you really miss your momma. I love you I know and I will see you soon I know your daddy has been keeping you from talking to me but I will see you soon, Mommy loves you baby." the phone hangs up.

Dr. Mark Sand presses the garage door opener as if he was just arriving and not to make a scene from an obvious inflamed situation that he heard Rachel with her baby daddy over the phone.

Dr. Mark Sand enters the kitchen and sees Rachel she is obviously still angry and breathing a little hasty Dr. Mark Sand asks, "Hey Rachel, how was your day, and did you eat anything or cook today?"

Rachel responded, "No, Mark I did not and I am not going to cook today you just have to make you something to eat!"

Dr. Mark Sand replied, "Alright Rachel, you do not have to shout at me I have not done anything to you but walk through the door just now. I am going up stairs to watch TV, I do not want to fight with you tonight Rachel,

I am not in the mood. I know you had a bad day again and I know how you get and I do not want a repeat of last night. We can go and get the rental car tomorrow morning for you."

Dr. Mark Sand goes up stairs to the media room and suddenly Rachel comes up with the baby in hand and shouts, "Mark, you don't appreciate anything that I have done for you and I am tired of it! I am here all day with our child and you go off and work and have your life and I am losing myself here and you don't care at all Mark, you don't care at all!"

The baby begins to cry and crawls on the sofa chair. Dr. Mark Sand shouts back, "Rachel what the hell is wrong with you now!" I have come up stairs trying not to have an argument with you, it is obvious that I am not the cause of your anger today so who is Rachel?"

Dr. Mark Sand knowing that Rachel had spoken to her baby daddy today asked Rachel, "Rachel, who have you been talking to on the phone today and why are you so wired and upset at me when I have not been here all day to agitate you Rachel, answer me on that?"

Rachel pushes Dr. Mark Sand in his chest area and slaps his face and says, "I have not spoken to any one today outside of one of my girlfriends today Mark! I am not here talking to no man, I am here taking care of your child and not having a life you got that Mark!"

Dr. Mark Sand knew that Rachel was lying and he suddenly realized what the Bishop's prayer and words meant as Rachel continued to rant and rave about how unsatisfied she was and how she hated him and how she was so angry with him and her life.

It became evident clearly to Dr. Mark Sand that he was truly in the internal mist of his life and all love for

Rachel that was once there in his heart was suddenly gone and he no longer felt anything within.

Dr. Mark Sand shielded his child from Rachel as she charged him hitting him on his head and poking her fingers in his neck while slapping Dr. Mark Sand on his face and neck.

Dr. Mark Sand put the baby on the floor away from Rachel and grabbed Rachel and shouted in frustration, "Rachel, I know you had been talking to your baby got damn daddy because I heard you asking to speak to your child tonight and you just lied about it to me in my face! You now have the audacity to hit me and abuse me and I have never raised my hand to you or tried to hurt you at all, ever! You have no right to be violent against me; your baby daddy is who you need to be mad at, not me! Am I your punching bag of frustration Rachel?"

Dr. Mark Sand continued, "Rachel, you don't understand we are already divorced and I know you have custody of our child but I no longer care about that now, I will always be her father and love her with all my soul. I know I see what I see with you and I now no longer love you at all and I will never remarry your crazy ass!" Rachel came toward Dr. Mark Sand and slapped him again and pushed him in his chest toward the sofa chair and hit him in his mouth and busted his lip.

Dr. Mark Sand could taste his blood in his mouth and saw Rachel continuing to come at him to scratch him and hit at his neck, face and head Rachel kept saying, "You don't appreciate me, you don't love me Mark, God dam it after all I have done for your ass!"

Finally, Rachel took her finger and press it with great force against Dr. Mark Sand's neck and throat and Dr. Mark Sand felt the force and the pain of her anger and frustration in Rachel's eyes and the loss of respect for him as a man as she pressed and hurt his neck and face. "Ahh! God dam you crazy motherfucker it is over Rachel that's it, I do not have to take this stupid violent shit from you, and it is over between us!"

Rachel reached once more at Dr. Mark Sand and he felt a scratch on his neck and suddenly the chain around his neck broke one last time and in its place was a wound that bleed.

"Ahh! fuck Rachel, you crazy bitch! You have finally done it now, ahh shit my damn necklace you have broke it again and it will not be a third time Rachel!"

Dr. Mark Sand felt his anger rise and jumped off of the sofa chair lifting Rachel off of him and grabbed Rachel by her neck and placed her head to the wall. Dr. Mark Sand felt tears well up in his eyes and his fist was tight and he felt like knocking Rachel's head off from the feeling of frustration from what he had been through in this chaotic display of turmoil and relationship break down at this moment.

Dr. Mark Sand shouted, "Rachel you have lied over and over again to me and now you have done it to my face and even now you have destroyed everything in my heart for you and I know I don't deserve a life with you like this! I am not going to allow you to just hit on me and abuse me in my own house, are you crazy?"

Dr. Mark Sand's fist was balled up and he was angry at this point.

Suddenly Rachel shouted, "Oh yea, I got you mad now Mark, you made nigga, you just a fucking fat ass baby daddy just like a typical black nigga is on the fucking street you aint no different mutherfucker!"

Rachel continued, "Yea let me tell you something Mark, you want to hit me don't you, don't you Mark, well let me tell you something go ahead hit me nigga, hit me, go ahead and watch when I call the police on your punk ass, you want have your medical practice, your child or anything I will have it all nigga!"

At that moment, Dr. Mark Sand realized that this is exactly what Rachel wanted him to do and that was to hit her and lose everything as she would call the police and they would arrest him. Naturally, he would lose all that he had worked so hard for in his life; even his medical career but most importantly, his child.

Dr. Mark Sand released Rachel and saw his baby crying in the corner and picked up his child and went back down stairs and felt that a stranger he never knew was ruining his life and he felt terrible. Dr. Sand did not want to lose his child over a woman and an incident like the one Rachel just described to him and that was almost staged for him to react like a set up to be destroyed in his own house.

As Dr. Mark Sand finally arrived down stairs feeling horrible knowing his life would never be the same because he knew that Rachel had custody of the child per the divorce decree and he knew he would not be able to raise his baby from that moment on. He wept and tears came from his eyes as he held his baby possibly for the last time in his home that he built for his child to enjoy.

All this ran through his mind as he heard Rachel's footsteps coming down the stairs knowing that this would be her last day in his house and the last time he would know his child to live with him as a father. Dr. Sand loved and wanted his child never neglecting or abandoning the one child that he has always loved, even before the child was born.

To think that this heated inflamed moment could not get any worse, Rachel picks up the baby and says something that would drive the stake in the heart of any real loving man.

Rachel Shouted, "Mark, You know why I go home so much? Well I have a man back home that can work this thing out and makes love to me real good and your baby will play with his daughter when we leave and go back home, Mark!"

Mark was shocked and felt ripped from the floor of his heart and finally the tears dried up and the pain suddenly ceased in his chest Dr. Mark Sand, felt numb and all his sensations for Rachel came to a complete pause and all his emotions for Rachel suddenly left from his consciousness.

Dr. Mark Sand responded confidently, "Rachel, as sure the sun sets today you will be out of this house guaranteed and you will never be married to me again!" Rachel grabbed bread and crackers from the counter and stuffed the bread and crackers in the under wear and shorts of Dr. Mark Sand. Rachel said, "that's for your fat ass, you and your Momma, ya'll don't like me any damn way!"

The bread and crackers fell to the floor and Dr. Mark Sand picked it up with the dust pan and broom with a heavy heart all the same.

Dr. Mark sat in his recliner chair and he felt suddenly free of fear as he watched his baby crawling on the floor. Rachel came up on Dr. Mark Sand and said, "You know I was just playing right? I know you mad but I was just kidding with you, Mark!"

Kneeling before him Dr. Mark Sand felt nothing for her anymore and Rachel clearly saw that his face and continence was completely different and all his passion for her had left his soul. The Internal mist the Bishop warned them about had come to fruition and all Dr. Mark Sand could see of Rachel is the vapors of what once existed in his heart for her.

Dr. Mark Sand knew Rachel as a liar and he knew she was once again trying to use her sexual appeal to sway his mind toward her control over him once again as in days gone by. As Dr. Mark Sand, sat in his recliner feeling horrible inside hearing Rachel's false sexual interlude of affection.

Dr. Mark Sand Shouted to Rachel, "Suck my dick, you want me to bow down to you woman after what you said to me about fucking another man! You want to now sexually persuade me like some pussy crazed man for your ass, here is my dick, suck this dick Rachel!"
At this moment out of pure frustration and anger Dr. Mark Sand took out his dick and it was not erect just limp because he was not turned on at all; he was totally disgusted and angry at Rachel.

Rachel then said, "Well if you want me to suck it I can suck Mark but I want you to make love to me and I want you to know that I am not going anywhere Mark!" Rachel then proceeded to perform oral sex but sucked it only with the tip of it in her mouth.

Dr. Mark Sand shouted, "Rachel if you are going to suck it at least suck it like you want to make me feel good, so suck it for real or get your ass away from Me!"

Rachel then went down on his dick a few times and Dr. Mark Sand set back and knew he was only feeling her mouth on his dick and not her love for him at all. It all made sense at this point and he knew that he could never love her again as he kept hearing her admission of infidelity to him after all he had done to save his family with the Bishop's counseling, trips for money he had given to Rachel and even paying her mortgage.

As Rachel sucked his dick all he could see is the other man standing between him and the life he once wanted with Rachel.

Dr. Mark Sand's mind turned from anger to revenge and as he thought about revenge, his dick went from limp to erect in Rachel's mouth as she stroked his shaft up and down as to try to sexually over power Dr. Mark Sand's mind by giving him pleasure.

Rachel looked at Dr. Mark Sand and said, "I see you are getting hard now, I knew you would want me and not want me to leave, right Mark? I know you and I got you, let's make love Mark!"

Dr. Mark Sand replied, "Yea let's make love Rachel let's do it, yes show me how you make love to your man Rachel! I want to know what I have not been getting from you."

Rachel said, "Mark you are mad and I know you are but after we make love you will be back to where we used to be Mark come on lay down and let me please you." Rachel continued, "Mark let's do it like you like it, I will get on top and I know you like that." said Rachel.

Dr. Mark Sand replied, "Every time I have ever asked you to get on top you never do and now after all this shit tonight now you want to get on top Rachel, for what? What is different now Rachel? Is your fucking secret out now to me, huh? Alright Rachel, I am going to fuck you and I don't feel no love for this shit any more I want you to know that; you can tell your man that as well!" shouted Dr. Mark Sand.

Rachel got on top and perpetrated like she was having a great sexual experience with Dr. Mark Sand. The moment was quiet and without any emotion or connection Dr. Mark Sand for the first time looked at Rachel like she was a prostitute and only fucked her for revenge.

In his mind, nothing was there as he fucked Rachel just for the sake of having an orgasm like a casual sexual experience but no emotional devotion remained as he thrust his dick in her vaginal canal.

"Rachel, turn over as I hit it from the back too, I want the full treatment like you do all the time for your man, I want that too Rachel!" shouted Dr. Sand.

So Rachel got on her hands and knees doggy style positioning and Dr. Mark Sand put lubricating gel on his condom as he had a fully erect penis at this point. He thought about fucking a prostitute for sexual adventure but more importantly he was getting his last fuck from the woman that admitted to cheating on him and in that sense his dick was hard but revenge was the climax not the emotional bond at all.

Dr. Mark Sand penetrated Rachel from behind, as his nature penetrated her, it was as if he did not know her. He was only there to seek revenge and get back at a woman that has ruined his life and had cheated him out of raising his baby and worst has even admitted infidelity to his face.

Finally, Dr. Mark Sand told Rachel, "ahh yea turn over Rachel I want to at least get the missionary on tonight right, let's do it Rachel, let's do it!" Dr. Mark Sand placed Rachel in the missionary position and penetrated her once again in this new position with his condom on as he thrust inside her with all his might and Rachel moaned with her own twisted satisfaction of sexual pleasure.

Rachel actually begged for him to go deeper and harder inside her as she kissed his neck and kissed chest rubbing her hands on his back as he felt her finger nails passionately scratch him in the lower part of his back. Dr. Mark Sand shouted , "Ohh yea Rachel, fuck me right baby, fuck me right now give it to me, let me all the way in that pussy, Rachel!"

The soul of passionate love was gone between Rachel and Dr. Mark Sand as the two of them fucked each other with the rhythm of revenge and sacred satisfaction that was based on control of the prey and not emotional enjoyment of the moment.

The Internal Mist Syndrome was very apparent in Dr. Mark Sand's mind and even Rachel's as well. Dr. Mark Sand knew that trying to stay in this fake relationship while living in all this misery for his baby sake was too much to deal with in his heart.

While his baby slept in her crib and the two fucked like ravishing teenagers with no purpose of destiny involved, "Ahh! Ohh! Uh, uh oh yea that was good Rachel and it was our first fuck in this house between us!" said Dr. Mark Sand.

Rachel said, "yea whatever, Mark you know you liked this good shit, right?"

Dr. Mark Sand left the master bed room and went to bed in the guess room and locked the door behind him. The next day he and Rachel went and got the rental car.

Dr. Mark Sand got all of Rachel's clothing and put them in boxes in the garage. Rachel went over to a friend's house that night and came back the next day and ask to come in.

Dr. Sand let her in and suddenly Rachel said, "Mark, I am not going anywhere I love you and you are going to love me and we are not going to be apart from each other! I am not giving up my life with you and you will be mine and I am not going anywhere Mark, no I am not!" Rachel shouted with that statement Dr. Mark Sand and Rachel became violent where Dr. Mark Sand was determined to get her out of his house.

Rachel ran into the bathroom with the baby and locked the door and shouted, "Mark, I aint going nowhere, Mark you are stuck with me and I am stuck with you and I am going to stay right here, dam it!"

Dr. Mark Sand was totally full of rage and anger and just wanted her to leave and get out of his life. He felt terrible because he could hear his child crying and knew that he never wanted his baby to see this type of activity between himself and Rachel.

Dr. Mark Sand got a screw driver and opened the door and grabbed his baby to give comfort and he saw that she was scared with all the yelling and screaming going on.

Dr. Mark Sand took his baby and put her in the rental car and closed the door and the baby went to sleep. He came back in the house to physically remove Rachel from his house. Rachel ran into another room and locked that door as well.

Dr. Mark Sand shouted, "Rachel, you are getting out of my damn house just like I said you would, you are getting out of here today, right now!"

Rachel said, "Mark I know you are mad and you have a right to be mad but I didn't know you would be this mad Mark I am not going nowhere Mark, I am not going!"

Dr. Mark Sand had to get the screw driver again and opened the door and he physically grabbed Rachel and Rachel purposely fell to the ground and grabbed at the door and the furniture in the house as he dragged her out of the room.

Rachel pushed Dr. Sands and he grabbed her and actually tore her pants as he picked her up and carried her to the garage door and finally pushed her outside the garage door into the garage and closed the door.

Rachel screamed, "Mark, what the fuck, you know you love me why are you doing this I said was sorry Mark, I know you are mad, but I still love you Mark!"

"I do not love you Rachel and you need to leave and go back to Georgia!," shouted Dr. Sand.

A while later Dr, Mark Sand, had to call the Sheriff after he had bought a plane ticket for Rachel to have a flight home. Rachel intentionally missed that flight on purpose.

The Sheriff came in the house and asked, "who called for the Sheriff?" Dr. Mark Sand said, "I did Sheriff because my ex-wife is on my property and she is refusing to leave my home and we are legally divorced and she has become violent with me and I want her out of here."

The sheriff looked at the divorced papers and asked, "Dr. Mark Sand is this our house and does she have her own place of residence?"

Dr. Mark Sand replied "yes, she does and it is in Georgia and not here." Rachel interjected and shouted,

"Sheriff I have been here and stayed here with him because this Doctor invited me here and he is now trying to get rid of me when we have a divorce and were going to be remarried, I left my job and my child to be here; he even caused these bruises on my arm, Sheriff!"

The Sheriff interjected, I don't see any bruises ma'am and I hear what you are saying ma'am but I am not a judge or jury, I can only enforce the law and according to the law, Dr. Sand is the legal owner of this property and you do have your own place of residence out of state according to your divorce. He has even bought you a rental car and a plane ticket home. Why are you still here right now ma'am, you are illegally trespassing, right now?"

The sheriff closed the door and said to Rachel, "Ma'am, you are trespassing and if you do not leave here legally, you have 5 minutes to leave these premises or go to jail for trespassing. Now, I do not want to do that but you are in violation of the law if you stay here illegally on this property."

Rachel asked, "Well, can I at least get a shower before I leave?"

The Sheriff replied, "that's up to Dr. Sand but you remember if I have to come back here for any dispute you are the one that is trespassing ma'am, take the plane ticket and leave these premises today."

The Sheriff left the house and Dr. Mark Sand felt relieved finally it was over. Rachel took her shower and finally got the last of her things she could carry for her and the baby.

Dr. Mark Sand held his baby and kissed the baby and said, "Daddy loves you baby and I will always love you now and always."

Rachel and the baby got into the rental car and drove away with the second plane ticket that Dr. Mark Sand bought that day.

Finally the Internal Mist was over and fear was gone. Dr. Mark Sand took care of his baby and replenished the furniture in Rachel's house and provided more than child support and even kept Rachel and his baby on his health insurance plan to show that he wanted her life to go on until she could find a job and get back on her feet. The Internal mist was over and life would never be the same for either Dr. Mark Sand or Rachel. But at least there was finally a peace in life after the Internal Mist had finally cleared. Dr. Mark Sand accepted his role as father ever presents in his child's life while picking up the pieces in his own private life, as new day began again.

Chapter 4

Symptoms of Frustrated Men, modern day dating, before marriage and after divorce

In this chapter we will evaluate one of the most un talked about circumstances that many women have been in and out of with relationships. One thing most women all share in common and want to know is what's going on in the mind of a man that seemingly has it all money, looks, career and the nice house. However, when it comes down to commitment and stability in a relationship there is a disconnect from the mind of most men from women. I do not have all the answers to most folk's issues economic or personal. But, I can tell you this that many men have a respect level of selfishness that makes every man want his level of respect from a woman. If a woman does not meet that level of respect that the man is expecting from a woman, then the man will not respond to this woman that wants this man's affection.

Women have been trying to figure men out for centuries and vice-versa. It is the oldest most common path of all cultural patterns of humanity to try to figure out what the opposite sex wants and how to deliver on those desires without looking desperate for love or anxious for sexual pleasure.

Quite frankly, the truth is, both traits of human nature apply we are programmed by nature to be curious of the opposite sex and inherently everyone is susceptible to the drive of sexual pleasure and intimacy of satisfaction from another human being of the opposite sex. This creates the paradigm of man seeking woman and woman seeking man this is played out in music, perfumes, fancy letters and even clothing that accessorizes our coveted sexual body parts.

I am amazed when I watch TV that the commercials show an attractive long haired vixen with the illustrious clothing and scenes of beautiful thighs and breast cleavage that will prompt any mind swayed by temptation. These scenes of arousal put our thoughts of into a frenzy of coveted passion for what most men and women will never be able to obtain in a life time.

This is what transcends the conversation into what makes men and women so frustrated when it seems that there is more sexual opportunity now than ever before. For example, the internet porn industry alone is just a click away from visually seeing the images of fantasy and human nature in its rawest form.

The question becomes then why do we look at internet porn? Most men have said the reason they look at porn because it lets them see a fantasy of what they wish to happen with them acted out on screen in the privacy of their own homes.

With this freedom, why would men be frustrated, the likely hood that many men become frustrated with women while seeking visual stimulation over physical stimulation often because most men feel that dealing with women has become expensive, stressful and in some cases even void of passionate satisfaction.

Men express a great lack of respect to express their sexual desires being ridiculed for what turns a man on. This is a great place to talk about one of the unique signs of frustrated men as it deals with the TV/internet and what is seen is not always what you can get.

First, men are creatures of visual and physical stimulation, I feel this is evident on the walls of the Great Egyptian empires and all through Great Kushite cultures that drew man and women in all kinds of sexually described fashions and styles on papyrus scrolls to show the illustrations of sexual intercourse and the satisfaction that was derived from the sexual interludes of the sexes.

This is still done in modern times from major magazines like playboy, hustler, hardcore and the mother of them all now of course, the internet. The point of frustration of men now is what most men fantasize about is not what they can experience in their lives. Now, this does not include the rapist, or the child molesters of society. This includes, the men that simply love what they see but are withheld from the forbidden fruit of passion by the law of see but don't touch in modern day society.

I must tell you that when men see fine beautiful vixens in the movies or even more realistically at strip clubs or tity bars as they are sometimes referred to; men want to play with what the male psyche loves to lust for in the inherent ability of manhood.

When a man is withheld from what he sees as tempting and alluring to his nature it is incredibly frustrating. Men are not the only sex that exudes this behavior women do the same for a man that the female craves as well. Women are better in my opinion of getting what they want sexually and drive men in sane for the ultimate climax to all men and that is with the vagina and the sacred fountain of passion commonly known as pussy, to most men.

All men are susceptible to good pussy like the cartoon character superman is to kryptonite. In this process of thought all men really love intimacy of what they have imagined from childhood by looking at their dad's or uncles old porn magazines or just simply curiously browsing the internet itself.

However, when what is in the media is not in the reality of the average male in America; the average male is understandably sexually frustrated. This is seen in males who will never get a cosmopolitan beautiful woman to have sex with. In contrast, all the tabloids, movies and internet porn sites show seemingly average men getting lovely natural 10 rated females that are vixens on screen, having casual sex with the girl next door as easy as walking the dog.

However, in reality in most men's lives there is a thing called, life and work stress. Naturally, the principles of this law of see but don't touch, look but don't stare and the American favorite, touch but don't handle; has been the subject of debate between the sexes for generations and has labeled many males as dogs. To the contrary, the psyche of the sexual nature of men is to touch, taste, feel and even become sexually promiscuous with many females over the planes of Africa and Europe as man evolved thousands of years to modern man of today.

As you can see for the American male it is easy to see why so many males love to watch porn because of the illusion of manly nature on the TV/internet screen is now the closest thing to the ancestral nature of early encounters of sex that real men naturally crave by nature. Modern time laws and economic demands cause frustration to escalate when men want to participate with women consensually in natural ways for sexual pleasure.

From this perspective, the evolving male nature, touching, feeling and exploration of the male sexual psyche for women over many thousands of years in evolution is nature's way to sexual exploration of the sexes. In contrast to the modern laws of today this may help to explain the frustrations of men before marriage and unfortunately after divorce.

One other sign of frustration with men is the social dating internet scene that often is a great game changer from the original dating scene of going out to a bar or even blind dating. Sometimes friends or colleagues will try to hookup a person by introducing a man to a woman based on some characteristics of things working out between them. This sometimes is a great thing but can be horrible in many ways as well when the relationship does not produce itself from such a meeting of two so-called like minded people.

The reason social dating can be just as hard or frustrating to men and women is because many people often lie or deceive on who they really are on social dating internet sites.

For example, a woman or man may place a photo of themselves from 4 years ago on a social dating website and claim it is how they look right now. Obviously, attraction is going to be in our younger looking days and often people like to use those photos to attract more possible dates.

The frustrating revelation is when you go to finally meet this individual and someone shows up to the restaurant or bar that looks 5 years older than their photo and has usually twice the weight that had been claimed they had. It is then you feel lied to and humiliated even as if you have met a total stranger. Many men have experienced this and felt totally frustrated from the internet dating scene. Comparatively, women I am sure have been equally frustrated by this fake attraction waste my time phenomenon, but I guess we are all trying not to be lonely in a highly social world these days. I have found another area of frustration for men is when you take a woman out on a date and the woman you take out on a date abandons you in the middle of nowhere. I must tell you, I have had this happen to me and it was not cool.

What makes this so frustrating is the fact that many men see this as disrespectful and the ultimate sign of humiliation toward any man's ego and psyche as well. This act of disrespect makes men who have suffered this act of selfish abandonment withdraw from women and do not want to trust them. In fact, a frustrated man wounded from this type of humiliation will put a mental wall up to protect himself from this event again; sadly, even with his spouse or trusting girlfriend.

Moreover, men with the heart to do good will abstain from social events in the dating scene because of the deceptive tactics some trifling women did to men that are not mature about respecting a man at all.

Believe it or not men love women to introduce them to their friends and colleagues. This makes him feel apart of the woman's world and this increases his trust in her and allows the bound of friendship to blossom even more into a better relationship in the future.

I have found in my research of talking with men that men become suspect of a woman that cannot introduce him to her friends or colleagues especially when the man is out with his lady friend. None of the men that I interviewed thought it was an okay thing for a woman not to introduce the man to her friends. I am sure women feel the same and I feel they should feel the same in this area as well. The secret to the man is to respect him and vice-versa for a woman. Just like men, women want to be praised and adored by the entertaining man with her and so do men that choose to be the date or the man by your side.

It seems if more people would learn that special skill of making the one you're with feel like a million dollars then you want be getting too much change in your life if you invest in your man and like wise men in your woman. I swear it does keep a lot of damn frustration down for real between the sexes. The great Otis Redding said, "Try a little tenderness"

The great Aretha Franklin said, "RESPECT". I think all people both men and women should learn about your partner and how to stroke the ego and not beat it down to get the affection from the man or woman in your life.

I think all men would agree with this sign of frustration and that is when a woman wants to move from a friendship into a relationship and the man is not ready for a relationship yet.

This can present many problems with men that can lead to men withdrawing from this very dominate strong willed type of female. One of the most frustrating commits that I have ever been told by one lady is, "You know Dr. Bell, I think the man is supposed to be chasing the woman all around town, the man is supposed to be doing all the phone calling for some attention from the woman. I am from the old school and men if they want my attention and affection are going to have to get down and do what I think they should do to get me Dr. Bell."

The woman looked at me and I looked at her and I said, "ma'am, have you ever been with a man for over a year's time or ever married to a man?"

The woman responded, "No, I have not but I would like to be married one day."

My reply was, "ma'am with your attitude and judgment of a man to a woman it's no question why you are by yourself. No woman can make a man choose her in his heart. Men love women who are natural lovers and exalters of the man they feel close to out of respect for the man they court or date, not demand of his affection. Any woman who demands or categorizes her man's affection toward her is already blind by her own selfishness. Quite frankly, most men can spot that kind of selfish, independent minded broad anywhere, women like you merely want a slave but never a man to truly love you. Therefore, being by yourself is not uncommon when you are so independent that no man can be who he is to please you."

The woman got angry at me and walked away. I knew she could not handle the truth because most of her life all men bowed to her in her mind. However, in the end once her mission of independent dominance over a man was revealed to the man interested in her; he had no choice but to leave her alone.

If you find yourself arguing day in and day out with your woman or your man then you will understand why so many men chose this scenario as one that caused so much frustration. It is said that money is the root of all evil. But when you have a woman or a man that you are dating that every time you go out wants you to pay for everything and the woman or man being taken out never returns the favor and pays on some dates, this can be frustrating as well. I am not amazed why so many men chose this scenario as one of the top frustrations out there.

Many men felt traditionally when taking a woman out on a date to eat or to the movies that they would have to pay for this occasional rite of passage.

Most men understand that they will have to pay for the woman that they are taking on a date because no one wants to appear as a cheap date these days. Well frustration start in most men's mind when women do not ever take the man out sometimes. Now, I am not advocating that women have to start reversing the roles here either. If a man takes a woman out on the first date customarily he already usually knows that he will be paying for the food and entertainment. Lord knows on the first date if he didn't do that he will probably be on the channel 3 news of gossip with some fired up women out there before the night had a chance to end.

However after getting to know you and taking you out on some dates there should be sometimes in a relationship that a woman can take a man out and pay for his food and give him a nice night out. If your man is holding down the relationship and handling the priorities of his manly duties not only in the bedroom but also with trust and consistency to you as his woman; most men thought a woman showing some gratitude by taking the man out can be a great thing in relationships.

I have found that many men feel taken advantaged of when in a committed relationship that the woman always wants to receive but never wants to take the man out on a date sometime. In men's mind this can indicate that you have an undercover gold digger or worst someone that is inherently selfish and can not share with you equally to show some appreciation to the man to make him feel special. Men love to be asked out on a date especially if they are in a relationship or a great friendship with a nice female companion. A woman that can be spontaneous and turn the tables and show today's good man that she can be a today's good woman if allowed to do so will respond and the stigma of gold digger or selfish will instantly be withdrawn from a man's mind.

This dramatically lowers frustration and I guarantee when your man is bragging to his boys in the locker room or at the bar with the guys he is only talking about how you made him feel and I bet all of the other men are simply like wow, he got a real woman.

Women have so much power and seem to always wonder why men do not respond to their womanly style of doing things. I say do something different, take your man out or if you're interested in a man and he seems like a great guy, ask him out to lunch or to the movies with you and pay his way sometime. This is the gate way to a man's heart it is not through his stomach anymore.

In today's economy, most have to share the load with rent or mortgage and paying the bills. It can get expensive with taking someone out to eat and now that real men do have to pay the rent or mortgage, car note and even utilities. However, if a man is still living with his momma, you do not want that kind of man any way. You know he is totally stuck in the Willie Lynch doctrine of laziness previously discussed in this book.

I always advised any good woman get a man that at least has a decent job and some money and certainly his own car. We know in this economy that people have lost some jobs and hard times have hit everyone. But that's why the sexes in this new dating age must equally share the roles of taking each other out and enjoying the good in each other.

Life is quite frustrating when you cannot enjoy someone without knowing that the one you're with can at least take you out and treat you well to level the dating playing field and eliminating old thoughts of being taken advantage of. Commonly, never being appreciated is a big way to keep frustration in your relationship, find a way to turn old clichés to new opportunities for whom you want in your life.

Another frustration that men expressed is when women hang up the phone when a man is talking and do not call back to conclude the conversation with the man. Now I know what both men and women are thinking, the phone went dead due to low battery or the person you're talking to dropped the phone by mistake. But what if you have a woman in your life or man that when you are talking to them that the phone always seems to hang up on you just as you are into your thought of expressing yourself.

I don't know about you but that is damn right frustrating and it drives me crazy. I am right in the midst of my conversation, then silence from the other end. My battery cell life is good. Naturally, I think the woman will call me back but to my surprise no returns call within a couple of minutes. Now most men stated that this is very frustrating to experience. It makes them feel the woman is not into the man or she has someone that she is entertaining in her life outside of her conversation with you holding the phone. I had to agree on this frustration because usually when a man is interested in a woman she has his undivided attention and the man is usually trying to put his best communication toward the woman. But if the woman is not into the man to at least return a call to let him know that she is sorry that she had an important call on the other line or at least to say I will call you later that is a really insensitive person. Usually, this is a person that is quite self centered and certainly not considerate of other peoples time or emotions.

I am sure many will have various opinions but I agree with the men it is frustrating to learn in isolation that the one you trusted with your time is wasting your time by not being very considerate of you.

I say when the phone drops or you are placed on hold forever then drop them like they are toxic waste and get you a better lover or friend on your line and keep it moving this will certainly keep your frustration to a minimal and not have a you as someone's sucker of the moment.

A big frustration that men expressed was the frustration that the woman did not get along with their family or friends. Wow, now this is a huge problem indeed and this presents many issues in life when dating someone or getting serious with a woman or man and they do not get along with your family or your friends. What is a guy to do with that type of frustration? Well, I will tell you the family is a mainstay and they have been with you from the beginning especially if you have a loving family. The new woman or man is just someone that you have just begun to entertain and gives you that nice feeling and good sex, believe me I do understand. Unfortunately, if you are a fun loving out going very intimate family person and you have hooked up with an introverted secretive person that does not like your friends or family and most men stated that these women felt as if someone was always talking about them or had an issue with them.

The crazy thing is no one even knew them or even had a conversation with them. Ironically, it was as if the damn woman was paranoid of social life with people you love to socialize with and value in your life. I have to agree with the men on this one as well, this is extremely frustrating for one reason mainly and that is this scenario challenges your very personality and character of who you are.

Entertaining, this new woman or man that you don't know who obviously does not want you to be with anyone but them is crazy. I have to just come on with it on this one. Drop that crazy ass woman or man that is paranoid and tying to separate you from who you are and the people that love and care for you your whole life like your family and your best friends.

I feel this level of frustration is extremely high and has no level of resolve to it. It is almost analogous to cancer, to treat it you simply have to cut it out of your life. Some people are like that as well especially when your personalities are in conflict with each other and the family and friends are now the enemy of your woman or your new man. Whew, sounds like a mental case and you better get rid of that introvert right now or you may become selfish, lonely, miserable and prisoner to a deranged individual that wants to control you.

Sadly, this person does not enjoy you to your fullest potential with your family and friends. I can certainly understand how this scenario could make any man or woman obviously upset. But the twist to this situation is most men have said that behind closed doors the crazy introverts are usually good lovers and can put the sex down quite well according to most men. These individual woman personalities are under cover freaks and all men love a good freak; just keeping it real. Now we see why this is such a problem with many men especially. Honestly, as men we know that good pussy and a freak on top of that will make some men compromise on Mom, friends and family from time to time to get that good sexual feeling that is not good but it is true. Wow, it is always a twist in these scenarios somewhere, well there it is. Obviously, we have to talk about what we are going to do to get though this situation. Well when it comes to pleasure, I can appreciate how good sex can make any man consider keeping the sexual satisfaction and intimacy experience for someone who can lay it down. But if you have a true paranoid woman or man dating you that happens to be the freak of the weak but does not like your family or friends you truly have to make some reality changes in your priorities outside of sexual pleasure.

Pleasure for a moment is just what it is, it's a moment of pleasure but living after the moment is truly the reality factor that all have to face in life. If your man or woman cannot accept you including your family and friends and attempts to create a barrier between you enjoying your personality which comes from our family and friends then that moment of pleasure will now seem insignificant even worthless. This moment's value will never add up to the value of love, trust and unity that your family and friends can bring you your entire life.

Remember no one is going to love you or be there for you like your family and friends. Another major point of frustration for men is when they are in a relationship and it seems that there is an argument between the man and woman all the time. Men have voted this frustration as one of the highest frustrations on the list because this basically means no positive communication is in existence during these chaotic times between both sexes in the relationship.

It is evident that this frustration does also much psychological damage to both men and women, it is evident that most men who seek therapy from a marriage counselor in 2010 did it because of stress exhaustion from poor communication in the home with their significant other or spouse.

I can tell you how hard it is to have to go home and be afraid to go home because you know once you open the door to the house a flame is going to hit you. This anger or rage can sometimes be instigated to an argument even after you already had a long day.

I have come to realize in my own life that some women instigate arguments with men for attention from their men and men hate that. Unfortunately, a breakdown in communication due to tension and stress over money is always the biggest obstacle for most couples to encounter in a relationship.

It seems people argue sometimes as a way of trying to learn how to push your buttons to see how you will react in various situations, which in God's name, I do not understand. Now a natural argument is a lot different than an unhealthy argument any day.

A natural argument is something almost like a debate if you will, it does not happen all the time and it usually has a sweet feel to it almost a little charismatic jousting to make the couple see the benefit of working things out.

This is the healthy arguing that most couples I interviewed stated helped them stay together for 15, 20 and my longest married couple was 33 years of marriage. According to people who have been married over 10 years it seems that natural arguing has become a way of love and debate; not a sense of danger and tragedy that I observed in toxic arguments with couples appearing on the TV shows, to solve that get crazy attitude while in need of counseling. The key about natural arguing is that it allows the man and woman to state their opinion and each major point is debated, the positives and the negatives are evaluated.

In natural arguing there are no name calling or throwing things or any physical violence executed from the man to the woman or the woman to the man. As you can see this is basically differing of opinion but yet understanding the love and role of both woman and man in a healthy relationship to solve an obvious situation that arises in any marriage or relationship.

In natural arguing the situation debated or discussed is the problem and not the spouse, girlfriend, boyfriend or husband. The subject of the natural argument is the matter at hand, not each other. I feel that is a great point to stress because I don't know one couple I interviewed that did not ever have a natural argument.

In fact, one couple put it so eloquently, "we never had one argument, we have had several but it made us better because love and understanding was never what we argued about it was always the matter at hand."

I swear I learned so much from talking to them, I can clearly see that if a couple argues over a matter it is not unhealthy but when a couple argues consistently about each other; that's when toxicity of personalities clash and the love bank of communication is consistently depleted of affection for your significant other.

So it is good that many couples and men put this arguing thing to a systematic tangible understanding. I feel now that I understand healthy natural arguing and unhealthy toxic arguing but how does unhealthy arguing affect the relationship where the man and woman go from love to hate in a matter of time?

One example, how unhealthy arguing or toxic arguing can ruin a relationship is with the name calling and bringing out the negative that someone has done in the past like a whip to mentally beat them with it almost to try to control them psychologically. This can cause any man or woman to totally dislike their significant other or spouse and it depletes the interest of attraction for who you once cared for in your life.

I can clearly see now how men and women can rationally begin to pull away from a relationship when going home is a consistent torment of badgering name calling and self destructive accusations that can sabotage any good and decent hearted individual. Now add on the chaos of disrespect and the toxic communication that paralyzes anyone from being heard in a negative firestorm of noise without any rationale at all just simply arguing constantly. As one couple put it, "Arguing from sun up to sun down even at breakfast, lunch and dinner. No harmony, no laughter or joy and above all no sweetness to each other; yet, the heart is constantly aching inside from this desert of a decaying toxic relationship."

Wow, that is hard to imagine in a relationship where love once existed and all things of joy that once was there is now all fading away. The noise of unhealthy communication where fussing and verbal fighting are a daily routine of life and behind closed doors from the public is a prison of despair, rage, mental abuse and isolation with deep regret to sometimes life itself. I can truly see now why divorce can truly be an option to many people who have tasted the bitter cup of this violent place of communication rage. According to most men, it seems that infidelity or cheating was never on a man's mind until going home became so uncomfortable that being away from home with another woman was an oasis from the rage of being home.

What alarmed me was when women and men say that having an affair was the farthest thing from their minds until toxic communication forces the heart to look outside the walls of home. Unfortunately, home life has become that toxic from violent and isolating toxic communication at home. It seems that men and women are not meant to argue like that to where home is not even home any more to either party.

In fact, even the Holy Bible jumped in this discussion from one of my married Pastoral couples that pointed out in the book of Proverbs chapter 21 verse 9 states, "Better to dwell in a corner of a housetop, than in a house shared with a contentious woman." Chapter 21 verse 19 states, "Better to dwell in the wilderness than with a contentious and angry woman."

Wow, do I need to say more than that, I mean that came from the word of God the Holy Bible. So men I feel you on this one right here. I guess it is better to divorce and be alone in the wilderness than to be with one of these hot angry self centered women that love to argue, all the damn time.

That being said, men if you are the contentious man playing the role of a bitch in the relationship then I have to be real and certainly see where the women may want to get out of this type of toxic relationship as well.

I swear, I have never looked at arguing today as I see it right now and I can see it from a man's perspective being a man but I feel I can understand things from the female perspective as well. It seems that there are two forms of arguing in a relationship or in marriage. One form is positive and nurturing while the other is toxic and risk damaging communication and destroying the love you may have for your significant other or spouse. I know if I ever get married again, I will seek the nurturing communication most certainly; it is evident that all couples argue but most do it nurturing each other and learning each other but never arguing at each other or destroying the union of trust and communication for each other.

As a man, I can understand that there are two sides to every argument but I can clearly see that if both sides are in a firestorm and no one is damping down the fire or worst the toxic level of understanding is void from reason that it is better to be in the wilderness or even on the house top than to be in the home with a consistent contentious angry woman or man. In other words, get the hell out of that crazy situation and find yourself some peace of mind from that toxic relationship.

It seems that we have covered some core frustrations that men have expressed with me over the years but one yet remains that many men my age 40 and older have expressed with entering the dating scene of today and that is dealing with the children of today with dating now at the age of 40. I swear so many men fear this more than anything and that is falling love with a woman who is so cool and great but when you meet her kids it is like little terrorist coming out at you. It is a razor edge walk of frustration when the children have been raised very loosely if I can say that and have no proper home training at all. I was saying if I was a woman and wanted to date

I would make sure that my home life was in order and my children were well behaved.

Many men had so many horror stories of frustration from this point of view that it has put me on guard when dating women with kids. I swear it has because now I am divorced and now I am open to the dating scene but I too have a child now, so I have to tread softly with the kid issue.

I don't judge women or men with children because I would be judging myself because I am a parent also. But I know if children are not reared well this can present a problem to any man entering this type of undisciplined home.

Many men always state that the heart of any home is how well it is governed prior to them entering into the relationship with a woman. In other words, before a man comes into a woman's life she should already have home intact and children organized with proper child rearing so they can follow proper authority. This limits events of havoc in the home if a man desires to come into such a relationship where children already exist.

It is my opinion that if a man does not have children then he should seek a woman without kids to start his life out with no matter how old the man is. I can tell you from experience that there will never be a shortage of woman without children for an older man with no children to start life out with.

Do I ever wish that I could have had this wisdom some years ago? Yes, that is the blessing in life, to live and learn while trying to inform and make aware the youth who are seeking advice about what others have gone through. You can always refer to my first book Invasion of the Baby Daddy to get a clear view of this type of breakdown in relationships that have kids involved. Unfortunately, the statistics are not good on the side of African-American men because the generations now are very promiscuous and have children early in life. In comparison, by the age of 32 the majority of African-American women have had at least one child.

Therefore, if you are a late bloomer of a male and are looking for a female by age 35 you better really look extremely carefully because the pool of women without children exist but it is also smaller as you get older, just keeping it real.

Furthermore, no matter how many women have kids It means men have them too and we men have to be responsible for our kids and be a part of their life. I for one have to see my own child regularly and make sure she has child support and gets to know me as much as possible.

Now I and her mother get along and I still love her but make no mistake, I am not in love with her any longer as a husband to a wife but I am not going to dog her out either.

Now men, let's be real if you are dogging your woman out then that also is saying something about you and you have to answer for that with your child as they grow up. That may not be so kind in the future with the seeds of abuse and evil deeds that you lay down with your baby momma today.

I have found that if a man is being a part of his child's life and not with the mom that is great, no harm no file that should be a great situation. In contrast, if a woman is yet arguing and having divisional tactics with the baby daddy in court and this is being played out over the children, who are caught in the middle of this family feud;

advisedly, men do not enter into these types of relationships.

Quite frankly, most men think they are going to save the day but you will not and unfortunately this type of family structure is doomed to always have conflict and the only ones that get hurt in these wars of irresponsibility and ignorance are the kids and that is a damn shame.

Children are always innocent in these frustration confrontations but over time they act out for attention of both the biological parents to secure their love. Furthermore, it becomes a real behavior issue for the incoming man or woman that has to deal with the psychological damage that both biological parents instill in their child's fragile personality and this acting out presents aggression and disobeying behavior that many men and women fear when entertaining someone that has a child that has dealt with a toxic relationship.

In my own life, I try never to argue with my ex-wife especially in front of our child it is this principle that let me see that divorce and living apart was best for me and my ex-wife. I knew it would mean a better home life of civility for my child's psychological development; granting me quality time with my baby as well as a father without the frustration of past clashes with my ex-wife.

I can truly understand this frustration and it is very real every day with me. But if you have a child, take care of it and be responsible to put your child first in your life. Never compromise the time with your children for the infatuation of pleasure with another, this only promotes the cycle of behavioral problems in your child and can cause serious repercussions to evolve in the future.

I feel that society is getting better with addressing the needs of children and their behavioral approaches between blended parents and even separated or divorced parents. Let's keep it real it is a part of our society that most marriages about 50% within 5 years will end in divorce and that is sad but also it is reality today in American social culture.

I still say that if you spend time with a woman and you see that child is behaving irrationally and the woman neglects the child; advisedly, man run away don't walk, this is a disaster waiting to inflict on you. Just keeping it real, even the bible itself weighed in on this cultural abnormality. The Holy Bible (KJV) in the book of Proverb's chapter 22 verse 6 reads, "Train up a child in the way it should go and when he is old he will not depart from it." Proverb's chapter 22 verse 15 reads, "Foolishness is bound up in the heart of a child; the rod of correction will drive it far from him."

Proverb's chapter 23 verse 13 reads, "Do not withhold correction from a child. For if you beat him with a rod, he will not die." Proverb's Chapter 19 verse 18 reads, "Chasten your son while there is hope and do not set your heart on his destruction." Proverb's Chapter 29 Verse 17 read, "Correct your son and he will give you rest; Yes, he will give delight to your soul." Proverb's Chapter 17 verse 25 reads, "A foolish son is a grief to his father. And bitterness to her who bore him." Lastly Proverb's Chapter 13 verse 24 reads, "He who spares the rod hates his son, but he who loves him disciplines him promptly."

Wow, I am sure after that 3,000 year old Biblical lesson passed down from the wisest man in the world according to the bible King Solomon; one must agree that our American culture has strayed quite far from the precepts and concepts of good quality parenting at its best. Therefore, I must agree and understand men now more than ever about frustration with unruly kids in a home that can bring terrible consequences because the mother of that child is not doing her part to rear the child in a positive way in preparation for a good man and a stable relationship.

Men who have a child also should bare a great responsibility to raise the child. If a man does not become a father to his child and discipline his seed according to the biblical knowledge, he hates his child. It has to be a bitch ass man to be a biological father and yet act trifling in nature toward his child by not paying child support and providing the mental guidance that all children need.

This Willie Lynch phenomenon is nothing new it is only the true reason why over 73% of all African-American males are in prison and why there is a 71% single Parent house hold rate in the African-American community alone. This number is growing because there is a 41% single parent house hold rate in the Latino community and 37% single parent house hold rate among White European Americans.

Therefore, all of American culture is feeling the pressure and cultural trend of this fatherless in the home society and there are so many variables that can lead to this increasing occurrence in our culture. It also explains why there is a 39% drop out rate nationwide in America among African-American children

However, if fathers would simply step up and mothers begin to rear their children with strict disciplines, hopefully future generations will not be culturally destroyed like Willie Lynch predicted. I don't point fingers at anyone in the area because I am a divorced man with a child myself but, I make sure I do my part to not only financially take care of my child but I also implement a routine strategy to see my child and remain a great part of my babies life.

However, I do not try to interfere with the personal life of my ex-wife. This is a great thing because it means you can take care of your own child, while not leaving that child void or disconnected from a father's love. The right balance must be established if you are considering taking on a woman that has a child or children.

Make sure there is not a court order that can prevent the woman or the children to move with you if you ever have to relocate due to economic reasons or better living opportunities. If the woman does have a court order where she cannot leave the state and the baby daddy has equal authority over his child, referred to as a "joint legal status" with the woman you are dating, I must keep it real with you, you will never have this woman to yourself and you will always be invaded legally by her children's father.

I am telling from experience walk out now and tell the woman the truth in your life because many women are not even aware of these state laws. Remember this is not personal to the woman but it is the law itself; nothing against this woman at all. Moreover, it is just a bad no win situation concerning you. I am sure she will understand because she is stuck in her situation you can still go and find a better one and that is from experience, just keeping it real.

If you want more detail right here go read my first book, "Invasion of the Baby Daddy". Make sure that the biological baby momma and baby daddy are not fighting in a continual civil war over their children. If any of this remains don't miss around move on for a better situation of a less toxic relationship. In my humble opinion, if you do not have kids look for someone who does not have children as well always start the dating life the way you want the marriage to be as well. I hope I have fully addressed men's frustration with women with kids.

The last frustration that many men wrote me about and that came up in many conversations I have had on radio programs across the country was when a good man provides everything for a woman. I mean pays the bills, mortgage and gets the hair done including the customary weaves as well. Take the children out and make sure that the home has what it needs only to have a woman that does not appreciate a good man's act of kindness to where the woman herself is not satisfied and complains that she cannot work but all the while does not have to work.

I cannot tell you how many good men go through this crazy phenomenon and it is nothing new at all. I could not believe that you can get a house, pay the bills and provide for a family and be home every night and the woman still complains about not being able to have her independence and feels that life is boring being properly cared for by a man. Men all over the country believe it or not have written to me and asked is this true of all women?

The answer is obviously not but if you get a woman that is an independent freak of nature and she feels that a man is purely for satisfaction and money then she will not have the cultural up bringing to know how to cater to a good man. In fact, most of these women who think like that have had no real father figures in their lives before and so the maturity of their role to abide with a man is totally absent in her cultural upbringing. Fathers are not only important to male children they are also important for young girls because fathers teach young girls how to appreciate the man in their lives and how to value a strong man and respect the manly providing nature of a man and the guidance of a man in her life.

In comparison, just as a young boy needs a father figure to know how to become a man; a woman needs a father figure in her young life not to become so independent of a man that she does not feel the need to have a man in her life as a provider and protector of the family which is the man's role.

Unfortunately, with a 71% single parent house hold rate many African-American men run into many women that are the stigma that the Willie lynch doctrine addressed and that is the independent phenomenon of single women don't need a man. Therefore, how can you appreciate in your life when you don't even feel that you need it apart of your life?

Consequently, we have an entire generation of women raised to believe that they don't need a man to complete a family and that is the craziest abnormality of our African-American culture that is a real shame.

Furthermore, when a real man that is educated, well in finances and wants to provide for the woman in his life; however, the woman has not been taught how to appreciate the role of a real man like a father figure in her life, this woman will resist this man. Consequently, this female will become suspect of his role because it is a role she feels she has to play to be a woman. Unfortunately, this clashes with the real man trying to play his role in the relationship.

Apparently, this is a dynamic in African-American culture that will rob another generation of healthy parents to raise a family together and that is sad. It may also explain why there is such a high divorce rate and a low remarriage rate amongst African-Americans specifically. Men and women must learn about their roles in a family structure and how they fit into a family existence. It is a challenging frustration that many men have said is like taking a woman to a nice house to live with no strings attached or games played.

However, the woman will look for strings and try to play a role of a man to be equal to him as a provider instead of understanding that her role is to help him in the home not try to outdo the man that is the priest and provider of his home. Some men have stated that some women have said, "Being at home with the kids and tending to the family and making a house a home for the kids and the man or spouse of the home is boring".

I almost fell out, I could not believe that some women would be so crazy to see being a help mate to a real man would be taken so ignorantly by some females in society that cannot appreciate a good man that is crazy.

Many of my White colleagues I interviewed have stayed at home wives and they do everything from cooking and taking care of the kids and the house runs well. Some even have home based businesses or part time careers that embrace the family structure and coincide very well with home life.

As one of the White couples put it, "I don't know how these women of today do it without a good man providing and a good mother to rule the house and keep all things organized at home with the kids and family. You really do need two parents, it makes life a lot easier and better for rearing children and education aspirations for a solid child hood in a loving home with both parents."

I can see how men can be frustrated with a woman that doesn't know her role, my advice is to ask God to send you a good educated woman that comes from a good home life that knows her role in life concerning family and even career life so not to overrule a man but to abide with the man as a help mate in life.

I had a radio call in listener to a radio show I was on ask me, "Dr. Bell what if a woman made more money than you make would you consider that out of her role?" I responded, "Of course not, I would embrace it there is nothing intimidating about a woman in a marriage or stable relationship where she makes more money than the man. That has nothing to do with her role as his help mate and mother of the family. Money does not switch out roles of the woman or the man it only helps to make the family have less financial obstacles to deal with."

I felt great about that comment last year because many men never heard it quite like that and I hope I helped the caller out with the question. The truth is if a woman makes more than a man in a relationship it does not mean that she is out of her role due to making more money she is still the man's right hand partner as his counselor, lover, advisor and mother to the family.

It takes a great woman to live up to these principles in any relationship but yet is humble enough to submit to being a good woman and providing motherly love and companionship to a man that makes less than her.

Men should not feel ashamed or intimidated with a woman that makes more than the man in a relationship. You have a duty to your woman that has nothing to do with money at all. You are the man if she is rich or poor, your duty is to protect and provide on your level.

Money can't determine that skill of a man so when you come home, love your family and be what the woman loves you to be and that is a man who can lead, provide and protect and reassure the family with your strength and dignity of manhood that plants so many generation norms in the cultural rearing of the family.

When two equally yoked people get together one male and one female who knows their role in a family structure, then money is not the understanding of their life together. It is only then that all things come together and over the course of the generations we can finally break the Willie lynch doctrine of family destruction that has existed for the last 299 years in African American cultural family life.

Chapter 5

Walking softly in life keeping my soul sacred, yet open to Love

This is a chapter that I have been really looking forward to writing. It is a chapter that presents the current angle that my life has taken to this point and I am quite excited to be here. I have been through a lot in my life as have many men and women have at my age. I am truly an adult now and I can't fake that anymore and if people are honest with themselves getting older and learning from life can be a very liberating experience in itself.

I have learned how to walk softly and not judge anyone's life that is in contrast to my own. It is so easy to cast judgment on what others do in their lives but that can also be a grave experience if a person is not careful about their words about others.

There is so much to experience now at 40 years of age that I could not experience at my younger ages. It is amazing to me that I am divorced, a father now and I have a great business and now four books written with three published thus far and that is a blessing. I actually put a CD out with about 5 songs on it. I am sure it may never make bill board ratings but I am so honored that it is on the radio playing all over the country and people constantly request it and I am thrilled by that.

I always think to myself that all I wanted to do was to put my songs on the radio. To date my little CD is on at least 12 United States radio stations and two international stations including the United Kingdom and Sydney, Australia.

I am happy in my life at the moment and it feels good to be at a place where I can live and enjoy life. I enjoy being a father and seeing my baby grow up and I am excited about spending this summer with my baby. I am learning how to take close guard of my family ties to my baby because as a divorced dad I try to involve my new life with my child and enjoy the great experiences that only strategic good living can bring to all people.

I am learning how to laugh and calm down from thinking of everything right now in my life. I am now praying to God daily now to watch my baby grow up and participate in my child's development to see what my baby's life choices will be in life. I can only hope that I have made a good impact and influence on her.

Life at 40 is really different in many respects from my younger days because I am more in control of myself now and I can actually see that I have really lived a complete life at my age and I have traveled and been blessed not to be poor or wealthy at my age now but extremely happy and content to live my life as a great person and contributor of society as a Podiatric Physician and Surgeon and a former university professor and now a book author.

I have served in the US Navy in the Gulf war (1991) observing life and death on my years aboard the USS Arkansas CGN-41 that was stationed out of Alameda, California. I cannot believe that I was actually under Mount Pinatubo the volcano, on the Philippine island when it erupted in 1991. I had to dig out of ash on the ship using my bare hands and a shovel that's how much ash fell on the ship the day the volcano erupted. I have walked on the Philippine islands and fell in love from the Philippine islands to Hawaii and even the Middle East countries like Bahrain and Dubai. I have visited cities like Perth, Brisbane and Tasmania in Australia.

I have tasted great food across America and had my heart broken several times and worked in cities like Aliquippa, PA at the Aliquippa Community hospital as a podiatric medical resident. I enjoyed my time there with great Physicians in Podiatry surgery that taught me great surgical skills and good skills about the business of the profession that I still use today.

I have survived my time in Queens, New York city as a surgical resident where I had my car broken into for the first time in my life where my land Lord stated, "welcome to New York." I have experienced the isolation of racism; I have also lived with the good and evil as a Podiatric Surgical Resident Physician while in New York. I have witnessed good people come and go and even observed professional people resign from a hospital position that was not corrupt at all but were merely targeted by the powers of arrogance and scandal that caused great distrust while I was in New York. I thank God I completed the residency program and I see that by all that I have lived through to this point in my life that I have been blessed and spared from many alternative outcomes that may not have worked out so well I my life.

However, I still love to visit New York sometime, it is truly a city of 8 million stories and a raw atmosphere that is always evolving where you have to keep on guard at all times.

As I have lived, I have dated fell in love and slept with many women of all colors, creeds and nationalities.

I don't say this to brag just to say that I have lived and tried to find love in life. It seems that often the women I thought that were beautiful would sometime really like me and some would not. I always thought I was too big, too Black or at times even too nerdy to get a nice woman to fall in love with me. Some women would say I was too orderly or bossy because I had to focus on my studies of becoming a Podiatric Physician and Surgeon in my residency program at this time in my life.

I am so glad that all that is behind me now and now it is just a man regrouping and wondering where life will go from here. It is very exciting to get away every now and then and go to a warm spot in the Caribbean. I always love to be able to just sit back and enjoy the blue water of St. Lucia or the US Virgin Islands and Dominica as well. I have visited St. Martin it is a fun island as well.

I am a helpless romantic and as I get older I can only hope that I always keep my optimism about life and the possibility of one day falling I love with someone who can really be a great asset to my life.

I am open to all aspects of color and culture in females. After what I have lived through I only look for the best in people and the great gift of life in love that only God I feel can truly give two people in love.

I have looked at Indian women, White European women and of course African-American women and Asian women. All these groups of women have some great lovely cultures and features that make them all quite attractive. I realize that my dating life now is increasing in opportunity and I am quite happy about that.

I actually joined an on line dating service at one time and it was a cool experience. I am no longer on the online dating services now but it was good to get out and meet new females. It was nice to change the setting of how I dated in the past and I felt I was keeping up with society and the social trends of technology that you do not have to leave your house these days to simply enjoy dating. The world is changing all around us and all the time.

It is important to keep a positive attitude and good decision making is a strategy that I am yet evolving into in my professional and private life. I am learning how to discern by asking the appropriate questions in my life. I would say it is like I have heard all my life about the mid-life crisis or awakening to the new advances in life. It is always the new things that take so long sometime to get used to.

As I have mentioned, I am divorced and available for the best that God has in store for my life. I am open for new adventures now in life that I never truly experienced before. I was asked by a radio listener about a month ago would I go out and seriously date a woman outside of my race.

Well, I certainly would be open to dating outside of my race and if I fell I love with an Asian, White or Indian woman I would not mind it at all if I felt God had truly put us together and my heart was totally secure with that decision. I have had to realize that there is a possibility that I may never remarry again but that is alright as well. I am not in a fast lane to reach a mile stone like I was on my first marriage. I thought when I first got married that I had to lock my life down by age 35 and start having kids as soon as possible, I was under the impression that I was getting very old and missing out on life. You feel like that just out of residency and medical school, I should have taken it easy and slowed down. Consequently, I found myself marrying a young lady that was a nice lady but her life was nowhere near ready for marriage and I did not know what to look out for with women who had kids at the time. Let's just say I learned a valuable lesson from all that experience in life.

I learned that you cannot marry anyone that you cannot see every day. I learned it is not a good idea to marry anyone that is not as advance in education as your level of education and you really need to research about someone's life thoroughly to make up in your mind that can say that you have seen the good, the bad and the straight up ugly in your special one's life.

I have learned that I have to take my time and truly ask God to send me someone that can share my entire life and not just the part that I feel that the person will easily fit into. I had a great friend of mine mention to me about a thing called soul ties. I had never heard of soul ties but her explanation was like this, "a soul tie is a person that you allow in your life that you share an intimate level of life with that usually is a sexual affair and the heart or soul can become quite attached to this person.

Ironically, one can easily get hooked on that person or emotionally attached. Therefore, if you did meet someone else down the road that special soul tie can be your downfall because you tend to return where the soul feels satisfied and this repetitive behavior can cause so many problems in relationships.

It seems that only a soul less person can have sex and not feel anything for the person that you are having sex with. I have to admit, I don't believe that I have ever had sex with any one without feeling something in my heart for the person and the experience that I had with that special woman as well. I realize that I do not want to contaminate my soul from being secured with the wrong female and attract some crazy deranged fatal attraction type of female.

God knows, I do not need to meet that type of female now in my life. All I want to do now is just have a great time and take it easy and enjoy the good things in life. I am so proud that I have a good way of looking at my life with a mature lens to totally evaluate my life. I also pray a lot these days probably more than any other time in my life.

I am beginning to want to work out more and eat better, one of my motivations is my baby and my desire to see my baby grow up and thrive as a good person life. What do you tell a generation of the youth as they are yet too young to even know what you are talking about or know what you are going through? I feel that is where I am yet evolving toward and that is excelling toward reaching toward the future to talk to my children and my grandchildren even before they are born to tell them that I love them and that through my decisions, prayers and hopes of the future that the good Lord above will bless them and give them a great life for my sake.

It seems life is all about the decisions you make and what you are truly man or woman enough to deal with in this crazy life we live. I hope that when I get up in the dawn of a new day that I feel renewed and ready to take on a new day to seek out new goals and seek new aspirations that might be on my agenda that was never there before.

I guess looking at my empty home in its current state, I always ask God to bless me to have generations to come through this house from my children. Even if I do remarry I would like to possibly have another child and experience the whole thing this time to fully know about pregnancy and preparing for my new life. I would like to be there from the very beginning, I missed out on that with my first child due to my ex-wife living out of state dealing with her baby daddy issues.

Adversely, problems existed before I even came on the scene that I did not know existed before marriage, refer to my book "Invasion of the Baby Daddy."

So I know if I do have a new love reenter my life then I will want to experience the everyday episode of affection that will not be robbed from me from someone's life choices. Beside's I realize now that God himself does not want people to be alone in their lives.

It is amazing that God would say it is not good that man should be alone in this crazy jungle of life that we live in. It seems so wild to look at my life after all I have been through and yet desire to switch gears toward being a father and healing from disappointments like divorce, personal failures and not raising my baby everyday in the house I built.

Hopefully my child will clearly see that I tried to fit the color of the Rainbow of life. I can only hope my baby likes my colors.

Note from Author

Please visit my website at www.drjohnebell.com

Also please check out my other books that are available on my website and at amazon.com, my books are as follows: Publisher: River House Publishing LLC

1.) Invasion of the Baby Daddy

2.) I think I can be a Doctor
(a children's book for ages 9 and above)

3.) Do I fit the Color of the Rainbow?

4.) Written but not yet published is a book entitled, "Blue Ball Syndrome Why Ordinary People become Sexual Players" Currently under review by Strebor Publishing. Let's keep this project in prayer.

Please join me on FaceBook at www.facebook.com/drjohnbell

Also to purchase my CD please visit: www.cdbaby.com/cd/drjohnebell

Please email me your comments either positive or negative and any radio interviews or speaking engagements please email me at jamarhouse@live.com

God bless you for reading this book and I pray you get a lift in your day knowing that you have made a lift in my day by reading my book. Thank you for supporting my other works listed above. I love you in Jesus name, peace be unto you, always.

Dr. John E. Bell

About Dr. John E. Bell

Dr. John E. Bell is a Surgical Podiatrist and former University part time Professor at Strayer University in Memphis, TN. Dr. Bell received his Doctorate Degree from the Ohio College of Podiatric Medicine and his Master Degree in health Services Administration from Strayer University in Memphis, TN. Dr. Bell lives in Memphis, TN and has 4 medical offices where he is CEO of Excelsior Podiatry Clinic PLLC, an accredited business with the Better Business Bureau (BBB) of Memphis, TN. Dr. Bell has been on numerous TV shows including: Fox 13 news Good Morning Memphis , Fox News in Baltimore, Maryland WBFF, I have been a guest on the Ion media network TV Channel show with Tanya Dallas-Lewis in Fairfax, Virginia. I have a current commercial on NCR 24 hour news channel WREGTV Memphis. I have been on the Jiggy Jaguer radio Show, and on the Georg and Nakisha Blog talk Radio Show, The Jay Blog talk Radio Show as well. I have been a guess on the Rev. Jesse Lewis Radio Show as well. I have been a guess on the Prison World Radio Show.